Chapter 6:
Who rules?

Chapter 7:
Health and medicine

Chapter 8:
Could you get justice in the Middle Ages?

Chapter 9:
England at war

Chapter 10:
Medieval Britain: what changed?

Introducing KS3 History

Thinking about History

Before exploring this book, take a few minutes to think about these questions.

- What do you think history is?

- What have you learned in History lessons before? Did you enjoy the lessons or not? Think about why that is.

- Have you read any books about things that happened a long time ago? Have you watched any television programmes, films or plays about past events? Which ones?

So what is history?

History is about what happened in the past. It's about people in the past, what they did and why they did it, what they thought, and what they felt. To enjoy history you need to have a good imagination. You need to be able to imagine what life was like long ago, or what it may have been like to be involved in past events.

What about my History lessons?

Your lessons are designed to show you how, why and when things have changed through time. For example, at one time the king ruled all on his own. He could do what he wanted. He might ask his friends and supporters for some help now and again, but ordinary people had no power at all. The king made the laws and everyone had to do what he said.

A few people were very rich, but most were very poor. The poor lived a tough life. If they got sick they usually died. If they didn't work hard, they usually starved.

But as you know, times have changed a lot since then. Today we have Parliament, elections, law courts, hospitals and education for all. We still have a king or queen… but they have very little power compared with the kings and queens of long ago!

So you must be wondering how these things have changed, and why they changed, and when. This book will take you on that journey of discovery… and hopefully turn you into a top historian on the way!

How does this book fit in?

This book will get you thinking. You will be asked to look at different pieces of evidence and to try to work things out for yourself. Sometimes, two pieces of evidence about the same event won't agree with each other. You might be asked to think of reasons why that is. Your answers might not be the same as your friend's or even your teacher's answers. The important thing is to give **reasons** for your thoughts and ideas.

How to use this book

Features of the *Student Book*, are explained here and on the opposite page.

Key to icons

| Source bank | Film | Worksheet | History skills activity | Literacy | Numeracy |

Depth Study

In each book, there is a mini depth study that focuses on a significant event or concept. These sections give you the chance to extend and deepen your understanding of key moments in history.

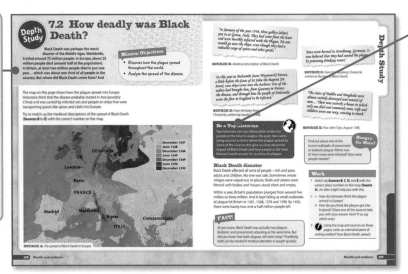

History skills

Be a Top Historian

Sometimes the tasks, ideas and sources will challenge you to think and act like a top historian and stretch your skills and abilities.

What Happened When?

This gives you an idea of what else is going on in the world (perhaps in another country on a different continent) at the same sort of time as the period you are studying in the lesson. It could also focus on a specific topic and make links across time, showing how things are connected.

KS3 HISTORY

Third Edition

Invasion, Plague and Murder

Britain 1066–1509

Aaron Wilkes

OXFORD
UNIVERSITY PRESS

Contents

Mission Objectives

All lessons in this book start by setting you 'Mission Objectives'. These are your key aims that set out your learning targets for the work ahead. At the end of the each lesson you should review these objectives and assess how well you've done.

Wise Up Words

Wise Up Words are the really important key words and terms that are vital to help you understand the topics. You can spot them easily because they are in **bold red** type. Look up their meanings in a dictionary or use the glossary at the back of the book. The glossary is a list of these words and their meanings.

Work

Work sections are your opportunity to demonstrate your knowledge and understanding. You might be asked to:

- put events in chronological order
- explain how and why things changed over time
- work out why two people have different views about the same event
- discover what triggered an event to take place.

Fact!

These are the funny, fascinating and amazing little bits of history that you don't usually get to hear about! But in this series, we think they're just as important – they give you insights into topics that you'll easily remember.

History Mystery

These sections give you an opportunity to pull all your skills together and investigate a controversial, challenging or intriguing aspect of the period, such as how King Harold *really* died at the Battle of Hastings or what happened to the Princes in the Tower.

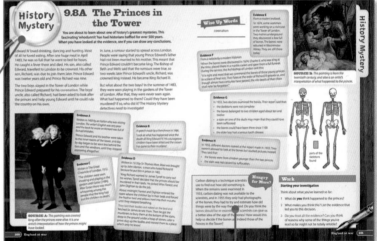

Hungry for More?

You might be asked to extend your knowledge and research beyond the classroom. This is a time to take responsibility for your own learning. You might be asked to research something in the library or on the Internet, work on a presentation, or design and make something. Can you meet the challenge?

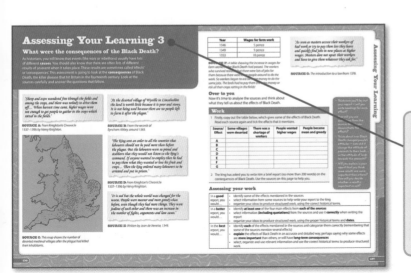

Assessing Your Learning

In the book, there are three extended assessments. These are opportunities for you to showcase what you have learned about the topic and to put your research and analysis skills to the test. Some are more creative, while some will focus on extended writing or looking at sources.

What is chronology?

One of the most basic ideas that any good History student must understand is something called **chronology**. Simply speaking, chronology is the study of when things happened. And, as you know, it's vitally important when studying history to know when things happened. Only then can you begin trying to work out how and why things happened!

When historians put events in the correct time order, starting with the thing that happened earliest, the events are said to be in **chronological order.** One of the best ways to show chronological order is on a **timeline**. These show the events of a day, year, whole centuries or even thousands of years, depending on the scale and length of the timeline. For example, the timeline below could be used to put your school day in chronological order:

8am	9am	10am	11am	12noon	1pm	2pm	3pm	4pm

And by changing the scale of the line, events covering a whole year can be added to the timeline:

January	February	March	April	May	June	July	August	September	October	November	December

221 BC
Building starts on Great Wall of China

AD 570
Prophet Muhammad born at Mecca

Around 2560 BC
Building of the Great Pyramid, Egypt

AD 793
Vikings first raid Britain

776 BC
First Olympic Games held in Greece

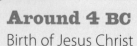

Around 4 BC
Birth of Jesus Christ

AD 1969
Man walks on the moon

AD 1415
English win the Battle of Agincourt during the Hundred Years War

AD 1666
Great Fire of London

Around AD 1300
Gunpowder first used in cannons in Europe

AD 1939
World War Two begins

AD 1485
First Tudor King of England, Henry VII

AD 1837
Queen Victoria becomes monarch

AD 1348
Killer plague, Black Death, reaches Britain

AD 1066
Battle of Hastings

Wise Up Words

AD   BC   chronology   timeline

Any length of time can be shown on a timeline. For example, the large timeline on these pages goes back to over 4500 years ago when the Ancient Egyptians were building their famous pyramids. The period in history covered by this book, known as 'The Middle Ages' is highlighted in the timeline.

Work

1 **a** What does 'chronological order' mean?
   b Why is it important for historians to get events in the right order?

2 Make a timeline to show either:
   a your school day
   b your life

   Try to divide your timeline into sections or chunks. Why not label your sections? Words like 'period', 'age', 'era' and 'times' are all common terms most often used by historians.

3 Think of different periods in history you've studied, perhaps at primary school. Make a list. Where would you put each period in the large timeline on this page?

FACT!

Historians use BC to refer to the time before the birth of Jesus Christ and AD to refer to the period after his birth. We don't know the exact year of Jesus' birth, but we use AD 1 to represent this time.

A journey through the Middle Ages

What's it called?

Historians (people who study history) love to give names to different periods of time. The 'Middle Ages' is what historians in Britain call the time from about 1066 (around 950 years ago) to around 1500. Another name for this part of history is the 'Medieval period'. In fact, the word 'medieval' comes the Latin language and means 'middle'. It's called 'Middle Ages' because this period of history comes between the ancient times of the Greeks and Romans and more modern times.

The Middle Ages

This book aims to take you on a journey through the Middle Ages. It is a remarkable period, famous for invasion, war, mystery, murder, revolt, plague… and more war! In fact, some of the battles and wars that took place at this time are some of the best known in British History.

During the Middle Ages, new discoveries and inventions changed the way people thought and behaved, whilst new laws meant that more people had a say in how decisions were made rather than it all being up to one man – the king. The landscape of Britain changed too. Villages grew into towns and London became a large and bustling city. The landscape became dotted with magnificent cathedrals, huge stone castles, abbeys, and churches, many of which can still be seen today.

Look at the timeline on these pages carefully – it shows some of the big events, ideas and discoveries of the Middle Ages.

1066

Battle of Hastings: William of Normandy becomes King of England

1340

The Hundred Years War begins

Black Death arrives in Britain

1348

1381

The Peasants' Revolt

Christopher Columbus (an Italian) discovers America. A new continent … and a new age!

1492

1485

Henry Tudor becomes King of England after beating Richard III at the Battle of Bosworth Field

1070s
Work begins on the Tower of London, one of Britain's most famous castles

1095
Crusades begin

Wales finally conquered by the English

1283

1265

1170
Thomas Becket murdered

1314

1215

Scots defeat the English invaders

The Magna Carta is agreed and signed

The first Parliament meets

1450
The Wars of the Roses begin

1453
The Hundred Years War ends, after 116 years

Work

1 **a** When were the 'Middle Ages'?
b How did this period get the name, the 'Middle Ages'?

2 Finding out which year is in which century can be difficult. The easiest way to find out is to cover up the last two numbers in a year and add one to the first two numbers. For example, 1348 is in the fourteenth century (cover up the '48' and add one to 13 to make 14)
a Which century are the following years in?
 i 1170
 ii 1492
 iii 1265
 iv 1095
b Which century were the following events in?
 i The Peasants' Revolt
 ii Signing of the Magna Carta
 iii The Battle of Hastings
 iv Henry Tudor became King of England
c Now put the four events above in the correct chronological order
d What century were you born in?

The **British Isles** (the correct term for the islands that make up most of what people call 'Britain') lie off the north-west corner of the European mainland (see **Source A**). Incredibly, there are over 5000 islands that make up the British Isles, of which only around 130 are **inhabited**. The two largest islands in the British Isles – Great Britain and Ireland – have the most people living there, but other smaller islands – such as the Isle of Wight, Anglesey, Jersey, Shetland, Orkney, the Isle of Sheppey and the Isle of Man – have lots of people living there too.

Mission Objectives

- Explore Britain's early history before 1066.
- Categorize early British history into different periods of time.

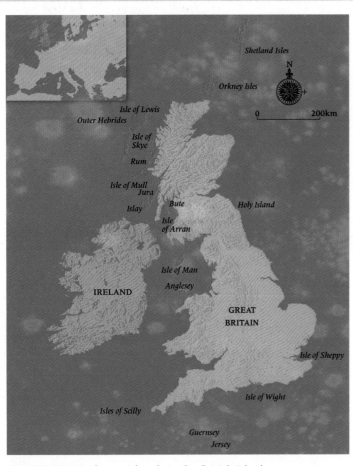

SOURCE A: *Some islands in the British Isles have very few people living on them – in 2007, Lundy and Piel Island had less than 30!*

So who lived here first?

We don't know much about the first people who lived in Britain. People didn't write things down back then, so most of our information comes from fragments of bone, bits of stone, fossils, pottery, and other artefacts. From these simple clues, experts have built up a basic picture of life in Britain thousands of years ago. But the picture isn't complete. There is still a lot we don't know. It's like an enormous jigsaw puzzle with most of the pieces missing!

The latest thinking is that for hundreds of thousands of years, there were probably no humans in Britain at all. But there were animals. These animals crossed over a 'land bridge' that linked what we now call the British Isles to mainland Europe.

Then, about half a million years ago, people from Europe began to arrive. These were Britain's earliest **immigrants**! They were **hunter-gatherers** who (as their name suggests) lived by gathering food (like nuts and fruit) and by killing animals for meat and furs. They moved around in small groups, sheltering in caves or building basic huts. They learned skills such as lighting fires and making sharp flint tools (see **Source B**).

FACT!

In this book, the word 'Britain' will generally be used instead of the term 'British Isles' when describing the nation as a whole. However, the main island is now divided into different countries (England, Scotland and Wales) and the second largest island (Ireland) is divided into two areas (the Republic of Ireland and Northern Ireland).

SOURCE B: *For thousands of years, hunter-gatherers could easily cross to Britain from Europe and back again because there was no English Channel. It was a period of Ice Age, so the sea was frozen solid. Then, around 8500 BC, the climate started to warm up and the ice began to melt. Over the next few thousand years, the land bridge gradually disappeared under water as the seas level rose… and Britain became an island.*

SOURCE C: *An early settlement. The one-room huts were built of wood and mud with pieces of turf or straw thatch for roofs. Note the crops in the fields and the livestock fenced into pens. Most of the tools people used were made from wood and stone rather than iron or other metals – which is why this period is usually known as the **Stone Age**!*

More settlers

For many thousands of years, life in Britain remained largely unchanged. More hunter-gatherers arrived from Europe and others left; some fought with other groups whilst others stayed isolated. Then, around 5000 years ago, an important change happened. People learned how to farm and produce their own food rather than having to hunt around for it. New settlers coming to Britain from Europe brought wheat and barley seeds to grow crops. They also brought animals for meat, including pigs, sheep and goats, and they owned tame dogs too. They built more permanent homes and cleared large areas of woodland for farming (see **Source C**).

Work

1 a Why don't we know much about the people who first lived in Britain?
  b How have historians tried to build up a picture of life back then?

2 a What was:
     i the 'land bridge'
     ii a hunter-gatherer
     iii the Stone Age?
  b What happened to Britain's 'land bridge'?

The Bronze Age

In about 2500 BC a new wave of settlers began arriving in Britain from central Europe. They were known as the **Beaker people** because of the decorated pottery they used (see **Source A**). The Beaker people knew how to make things out of copper and gold. When tin was added to copper it made bronze… so the time of the Beaker people is often known as the **Bronze Age**. Soon, tools and weapons made from metal replaced the ones made from stone and wood. The Beaker people also introduced the first alcoholic drink to Britain (a kind of beer made from barley) and the wealthy women wore jewellery, pinned their hair up with decorated pins and wore woollen clothes instead of animal skins. They may also have tamed wild horses for riding.

SOURCE A:
This beaker was found on a Bronze Age burial site near Haddington, Scotland.

After the Bronze Age

Over the next few thousand years, more and more different people arrived in Britain. Some came peacefully, whilst others were hostile invaders. Some came for only a short time but others settled for good. All of these new groups of people left their mark on Britain. Study each group carefully, thinking about how each group helped to shape the nation.

What Happened When?

800BC

Around 800 BC, people began to make weapons and tools from iron. As a result, this period in British history – up until the Roman invasion in AD 43 – is sometimes called the **Iron Age**.

The Celts

Around 500 BC tribes from central Europe, known as Celts, began to settle in Britain. The tribes fought brutally with each other… and with the tribes that were already settled in Britain.

The Celts farmed the land

The Celts built forts and introduced bagpipes to Britain

Celts wore shirts and cloaks that were colourfully dyed and embroidered

The Celts were proud of their appearance and kept themselves clean using special soaps and perfumes

Celtic priests (druids) were in charge of religious rituals. Some of their traditions survive today – Halloween and May Day, for example

Tribal business was done at yearly assemblies – land disputes were settled, accused criminals went on trial and people were voted into important positions

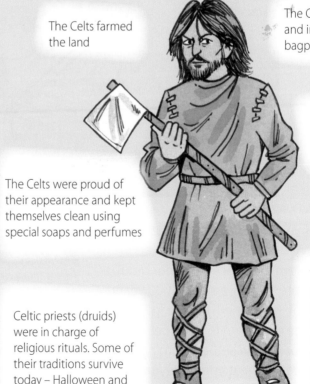

The Romans

The Romans, from Italy, invaded Britain in AD 43… and soon conquered most of the British tribes. The Romans stayed for around 400 years!

The Roman army was made up of Gauls (from France), Germans and Hungarians; there is also evidence of a Roman settlement of black Africans near York

Much of our language and some laws can be traced back to the Romans

Many of our main roads are based on old Roman roads

Romans were the first in Britain to use calendars, coins, glass, and bricks

Many Roman towns are still important towns today – for example, Chester, York, Bath, Gloucester, Lincoln, Colchester, and St Albans

The Romans introduced cabbages, peas, wine, apples, grapes, turnips, carrots, and cats!

FACT!

The Romans were the first people to use the name 'Britannia' for Britain. The name was based on the word 'Pretannia', which is what the Ancient Greeks called the British Isles because they thought a Celtic tribe called the 'Pretani' lived there. In fact, the Pretani tribe lived mainly in Ireland – but the name Pretannia stuck, and later became Britannia, and then Britain!

Work

1 a Put the following periods in history in the correct chronological order:

Bronze Age   Iron Age   Stone Age

b How did each of these periods get its name?
c Why do you think historians give names to different periods in history?

2 How did Britain get its name?

The Romans leave... but more invaders arrive

By AD 401, the Romans who were based in Britain were called back to Italy to defend their homeland from invasion. The British who had lived under Roman rule for hundreds of years were left to fend for themselves… and it didn't take long for new tribes from abroad to invade Britain. Around AD 450, invaders came by boat from Denmark and northern Germany and were called Angles, Saxons and Jutes. They soon became known as Anglo-Saxons, and after fighting with the British tribes, began to settle and live here.

SOURCE A: *This Anglo-Saxon artefact is called the Alfred Jewel and is made of gold and crystal. Around the edge it reads 'Alfred had me made'. A long stick fitted into the bottom. The artefact then became a pointer for following words in a book.*

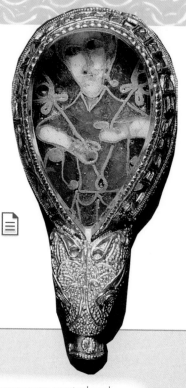

The Anglo-Saxons

The Anglo-Saxons drove many of the British tribes into Wales, Cornwall, Cumbria, and Scotland

Before converting to Christianity Anglo-Saxons worshipped many gods, and some can be seen in our days of the week:

- Tiw (god of combat) = Tuesday
- Woden (god of war and wisdom) = Wodensday or Wednesday
- Thor (protector of mankind) = Thorsday or Thursday
- Freya (goddess of love and beauty) = Friday

The Anglo-Saxons gave England its name – 'Angle-land', which means 'land of the Angles', later England

Anglo-Saxon is one of the key 'base' languages of English – bed, cat, dog, tree, lick, jump, hunt, fox, and fart are all words of Anglo-Saxon origin

Many of our towns were created and named by Anglo-Saxons – if your town ends in '-ton', '-wich', '-worth', '-burn', '-hurst', or '-ham' then Anglo-Saxons probably lived there originally

Anglo-Saxons were excellent farmers who grew rye, barley, wheat, oats, and vegetables. A good harvest meant food for the winter – and a bad one could mean starvation!

Powerful tribal leaders became local kings who fought other local kings to get more power. The strongest were called 'Bretwalda' or 'Ruler of Britain'. These included King Ethelbert (died in AD 616) and Edwin (died about AD 633)

Lots of our counties are named after the Anglo-Saxons. East Anglia is an obvious one, but others include: Sussex, the kingdom of the South Saxons; Essex, the land of the East Saxons; and Middlesex, the home of the Middle Saxons. Saxons who lived on the south bank of the River Thames were known as the Saxons of the 'south ridge', later Surrey

Here come the Vikings!

In the late eighth century the Anglo-Saxons faced invasion from across the North Sea by Vikings. The Vikings never conquered the whole of Britain, but took over much of the north and east, where many settled. A Viking called Canute even became King of England in 1016!

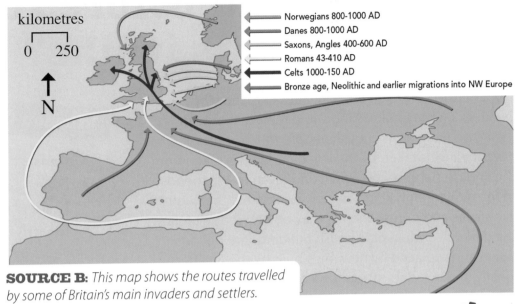

kilometres

0   250

N

Norwegians 800-1000 AD	
Danes 800-1000 AD	
Saxons, Angles 400-600 AD	
Romans 43-410 AD	
Celts 1000-150 AD	
Bronze age, Neolithic and earlier migrations into NW Europe	

SOURCE B: *This map shows the routes travelled by some of Britain's main invaders and settlers.*

From the late eighth century, Vikings arrived from Denmark, Norway and Sweden

Like the Anglo-Saxons before them, they were looking for land to settle on, but also for riches!

Some Vikings attacked and went home, others stayed – they settled in Ireland, Scotland and parts of Wales

Today, places ending in '-by' and '-thorpe' were probably named by Vikings. 'By' is the Viking word for 'settlement' and 'thorpe' means 'smaller village'

FACT!

At this time, the Scots (an Irish tribe) began to settle in what we now call Scotland. They fought with the Picts who already lived there. Eventually the tribes joined, but it was the Scots who the country was named after.

What Happened When?

AD599

In around AD 599, an early form of chess was invented in India.

Work

1   How did England and Scotland get their names?

2   Look at **Source A**.
    a   In your own words, describe the object shown.
    b   Think carefully, does the Alfred Jewel tell us anything about Anglo-Saxon Britain and the people who lived there? Give reasons for your answer.

3   Match the tribe with its description:

Celts	Arrived in AD 43 from Italy and ruled for around 400 years
Romans	An Irish tribe that invaded Scotland
Anglo-Saxons	Began raiding Britain after AD 800
Picts	Settled in Britain about 500 BC
Scots	A Scottish tribe
Vikings	Arrived from Denmark and northern Germany after the Romans left

4   a   Create a mind-map with the title, 'What did the foreign invaders and settlers bring to Britain?' Each branch of the mind-map should outline the contribution and impact of the different groups of invaders and settlers – Celts, Romans, Anglo-Saxons, and Vikings.
    b   In your opinion, did some groups contribute more than others? Explain your answer.

Imagine this: a foreign army invades England. The invaders kill the English King – and replace him with their own king. Most English people with important jobs have their jobs taken by the invaders. Land is taken from the English people who own it and given to the friends of the new foreign king. The new rulers treat the English like slaves and punish them if they object or don't follow the new rules. Most old English buildings are pulled down and replaced by new ones built by the invaders. Finally, the invaders introduce a new language.

Mission Objectives

- Find out how England got its name.
- Investigate what eleventh-century England was like.
- Identify who ruled England in the years up to 1066.

Surely this could never happen! Surely this has never happened! Well it did in 1066, when an army from Normandy (an area in northern France) invaded England. Not all of the things listed above happened straight away, but they definitely happened within a few years. Indeed, after 1066, England was never the same again.

But in order to understand just how amazing the changes were, and the dramatic impact they had on England, we first need to look at what England, Scotland and Wales were like before 1066.

SOURCE A: *Edward the Confessor, King of England from 1042–1066 is shown being crowned in this manuscript from the 1250s.*

Scotland was a completely separate country from England, ruled by its own king.

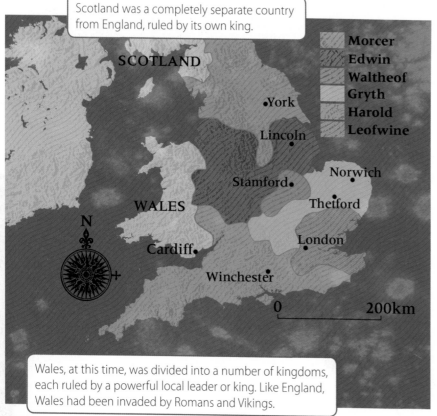

SCOTLAND

Key:
- Morcer
- Edwin
- Waltheof
- Gryth
- Harold
- Leofwine

• York

Lincoln •

• Norwich

Stamford •

WALES

Thetford •

London •

Cardiff •

Winchester •

N

0   200km

Wales, at this time, was divided into a number of kingdoms, each ruled by a powerful local leader or king. Like England, Wales had been invaded by Romans and Vikings.

SOURCE B: *A map showing the eight largest towns in England in 1066. The key also shows the names of King Edward's earls and the areas they helped him run.*

Who ruled?

By 1065, England was a country that contained quite a mixture of different groups whose ancestors came from all sorts of different places. However, despite occasional tensions between rival groups, England was peacefully united under one king – a man named Edward! (see **Source A**).

King Edward was helped in his role by lots of different people. Some were from rich, important families who looked after an area of England called an **earldom** (see **Source B**). But King Edward also took advice from some friends he had in an area of France called Normandy. Edward's mother was from Normandy and he'd spent lots of time there after Vikings had invaded and taken over large parts of England when he was young.

So how many people were there?

The population of the whole of England was about 1.5 million people. Nearly everybody worked as farmers on land that had been cleared but much of England was still covered by forests. People lived in small villages and probably spent most of their lives there. There were few towns – only about 15 with more than 1000 people living there. And only eight towns had a population of more than 3000 (see **Source B**).

Wise Up Words

chronicle   earldom   evidence

'The English wore short garments, reaching to the knees. They had short hair, their beards shaven; their arms covered with gold bracelets; their skin covered with pictured designs. Drinking parties were common and they drank until they were sick. Drunkenness weakens the human mind and they often fought with fury rather than with military skill.'

▲ **SOURCE D:** *A description of the English by a monk in 1130.*

SOURCE C: *This image from a medieval manuscript shows how farmers used to prepare a field for crops.*

Work

1. **a** Who ruled England in 1065?
   b Who helped him rule?

2. Write a sentence or two about how Wales and Scotland were ruled at this time.

3. Read **Source D**.
   a How does the person who wrote the source describe the English?
   b Do you think the writer liked the English? Give reasons for your answer.

How rich was England?

The rich were very rich and the poor were very poor. Out of every 100 people, about two were rich. They made their money from the land they owned (because people paid them rent to live on it) or from trading in all sorts of goods, some of which are shown in **Source A**. Some men made so much money they built fabulous homes and churches and lived in luxury. By contrast, life was very hard for the poor. Each family had to grow its own food – and there were no shops like today where we can buy more if we run out. If the harvest was bad, a family might have to eat roots, leaves, wild berries, and any creatures they could catch.

FACT!

Imagine your life being threatened by a graze or cut! People often died of small wounds and infections because there were few medicines.

SOURCE A: *This map shows the goods produced in medieval Britain and where they came from.*

SOURCE B: *Anglo-Saxon coins. The money system in 1066 was used in England until 1971. The currency was pounds (£), shillings (s) and pence (d). There were 12d in a shilling and 20s in a pound.*

Churches and monasteries Full of jewels and other valuable items, they were also centres of learning where monks wrote about famous historical events.

Fish Lots of fish stocked the seas around England.

Salt Cheshire's salt mines supplied vast quantities of salt, which was used to preserve food.

Wheat Wheat and other crops such as barley and oats were grown on England's fertile land.

Lead Valuable metal, used by the Romans to make pipes.

Wool Large flocks of sheep were kept and their wool and the cloth made from it were sold all over Europe.

Silver A precious metal, mined in several places in England. Millions of silver coins were used for trade.

Iron Used to make tools and weapons.

Tin Cornwall's tin mines are said to be one of the main reasons why the Romans invaded Britain! By 1066, England supplied most of Europe's tin.

Honey Produced all over the country, it was used as a medicine, an ingredient in beer and as a sweetener.

Copper Combined with tin to make bronze and then used to make tools and jewellery.

0   200km

N

Fish

Churches & monasteries

Salt   Wheat

Lead   Wool

Silver

Tin   Copper   Honey   Iron

SOURCE C: *A page from a monk's chronicle.*

Were people religious?

The simple answer is 'yes'. Everyone was a Christian and went to church. In monasteries (large buildings where monks lived) monks kept huge official diaries called **chronicles**. They wrote about religion, politics, history, towns, kings, gossip, and even the weather.

How do we know all this?

We certainly don't know everything about England at this time. However, we know enough to give us a good idea about what life was like. We can look at a number of different sources from the time, which allows us to build up a picture of everyday life – paintings, churches and other buildings, coins, weapons, drawings, jewellery, and books written at the time (see **Source C**). These sources are **evidence** of life in England in 1066.

SOURCE D: *The Anglo-Saxon church of St Laurence at Bradford on Avon, Wiltshire. As you can see, the church is very strong and may have been used as a fortress in times of trouble.*

Work

1 Use the information on these two pages to match up the start of each sentence (**List A**) with the correct ending (**List B**).

LIST A
- At this time everyone was…
- Monks often kept a record of important events…
- England was well known in Europe for its natural resources such as…
- Most people were poor and…
- There were some rich people who made their money by…

LIST B
- … renting out their land or by trading goods.
- … tin, cloth, silver, and lead.
- … Christian and went to church.
- … in books called 'chronicles'.
- … grew their own food.

2 Look at **Source A**.
   a What does the map show?
   b Do you think this map helps show why so many different groups invaded England over the years? Give reasons for your answer.

3 Use pages 16 to 19 to write your own fact file about England in 1066. You should use ten sentences to write ten different facts.

4 Some written sources in this book were written by chroniclers. These were men who wrote chronicles from their own point of view. They wrote about what they believed and felt, rather than what they actually saw. Why is it important to know this when studying history?

Who will be the next King of England?

1066 is probably the most famous year in British history. Many of you will have heard of it even though you haven't studied it yet. 1066 is so well known because it was the last time England was invaded and taken over by a foreign power. The English king and his followers were killed and the country was divided up between the new invaders. England's language, rulers and way of life changed forever. What a year!

Mission Objectives

- Compare the three different men who wanted to be King of England in 1066.
- Assess the three contenders and judge who had the best claim to the throne.

The old king dies...

In January 1066, Edward the Confessor, King of England, died. He was 62 years old and left no children behind. There was no clear **heir** to the throne. However, three men believed that they should be England's next king – and they were ready to use their armies to get their hands on the crown! Read through the fact files on each contender for Edward's crown.

The Englishman

Name: Harold Godwinson

Position: Earl of Wessex, one of the most powerful men in England.

Family history: His father, Godwin, argued a lot with King Edward. At one time Harold and his father were banished from England, but they returned a year later.

Links to King Edward: Harold's sister was married to King Edward.

Was he tough enough? Harold was a brave and respected soldier with a tough streak. In 1063, King Edward sent Harold to crush a Welsh uprising. The Welsh leader was caught and his head was chopped off on Harold's orders.

Support for his claim: He was the only Englishman claiming the throne. The Witan, a meeting of the most important bishops and nobles in England, wanted Harold to be the next king. English monks wrote: 'Harold and his brothers were the king's favourites... on his deathbed that wise king promised the kingdom to Harold.'

The Norman

Name: William of Normandy

Position: Duke of Normandy, the strongest part of France.

Family history: William came from a fighting family. He had been in control of Normandy since he was a young boy and was used to having to fight to keep his lands.

Links to King Edward: Edward had lived in Normandy from 1016 to 1041. When Edward returned to England to be king, William sent soldiers to help him. As a result, King Edward had promised William the throne in 1051.

Was he tough enough? His nickname was 'William the Bastard' because his father wasn't married to his mother. In 1047, people from the town of Alençon made fun of his mother's family. William captured the town and ordered that 30 of the townsmen be skinned alive.

Support for his claim: According to William of Poitiers, a Norman writer, 'Edward, king of the English, loved William like a brother or son... so he decided that William should be the next king.' Harold Godwinson had visited William in 1064, and may have told him this news and promised to support William's claim to the English crown.

Name: Harald Hardrada

Position: King of Norway

Family history: He had fought alongside several Norwegian and foreign kings and had taken part in raids on the English coast. When he became King of Norway, he began to plan a full-scale invasion of England.

Links to King Edward: None – but a Viking called Canute had ruled Norway and England from 1016 to 1035.

Was he tough enough? He was the most feared warrior in Europe – tough, bloodthirsty and he enjoyed watching his enemies suffer. 'Hardrada' means 'hard ruler' and his nickname was 'the Ruthless'.

Support for his claim: Harald's claim was supported by Tostig, Harold Godwinson's brother. The two brothers had fallen out and Tostig wanted revenge.

Work

Now you have read about the three contenders for the throne, you must decide who you think had the best claim (reason to be king).

1   Copy and complete the following table. Try to include as many reasons as possible.

Contender	Why they should be king	Why they shouldn't be king
Harold Godwinson		
Harald Hardrada		
William of Normandy		

2   **a**   List the three contenders in order of who you think had the strongest claim. Label your first choice 'strongest' and your last choice 'weakest'.

   b   In your own words, explain why you placed the three contenders in the order you have chosen.

3   Divide into groups. Each group should choose a contender (perhaps pull a name out of a hat!) for the English crown. Design a poster that will convince people that your contender should be king… and that the other two shouldn't!

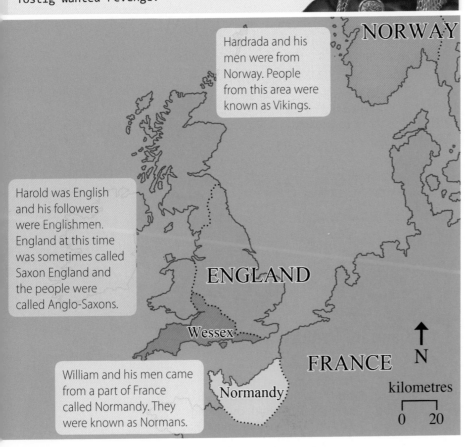

Hardrada and his men were from Norway. People from this area were known as Vikings.

NORWAY

Harold was English and his followers were Englishmen. England at this time was sometimes called Saxon England and the people were called Anglo-Saxons.

ENGLAND

Wessex

FRANCE   N

William and his men came from a part of France called Normandy. They were known as Normans.

Normandy

kilometres

0   20

The Englishman's advantage

When King Edward died on 5 January 1066, Harold had one big advantage over his two rivals. William and Hardrada were miles away across the sea while Harold was already in England. He wasted no time and was crowned king the very next day – but he knew that wasn't the end of it. The other two would soon hear the news and come looking for him – and they'd both want him dead!

14 Round 1: the Battle of Stamford Bridge

For nine months, King Harold of England sat nervously on his throne, waiting for his rivals to make a move for his crown. In September 1066 his wait was over. Hardrada, King of Norway, had landed near York in the north of England and he wasn't leaving until the crown was his. With him was Harold's younger brother, Tostig. Oh, and about 10,000 bloodthirsty Vikings!

Firstly, look at the map below to see how King Harold reacted to the news that Hardrada had landed… and then look through the cartoon on the right-hand page to see what happened when the two sides fought each other.

Mission Objectives

- Identify the contenders for the English throne who fought at the Battle of Stamford Bridge.
- Evaluate the physical and mental condition of the winning side at the end of the battle.

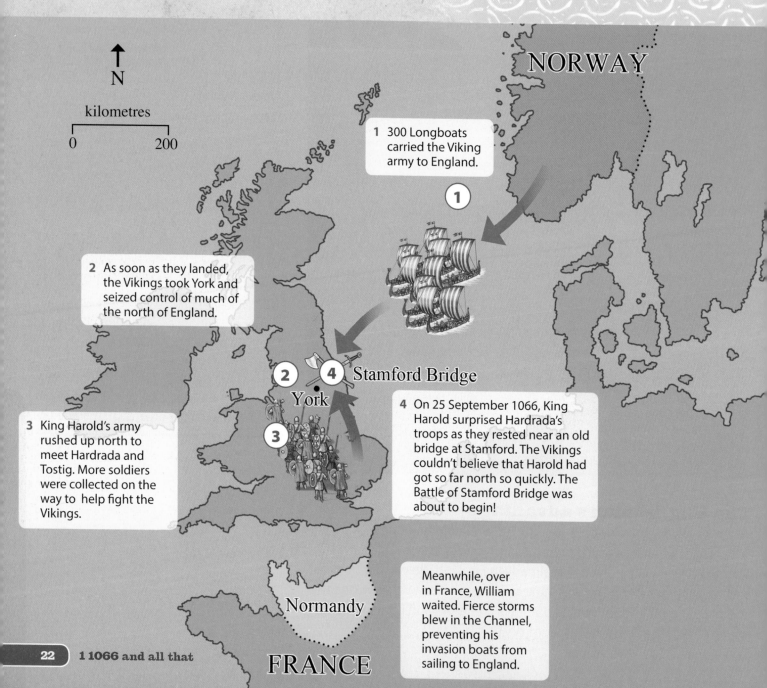

N

kilometres
0   200

NORWAY

1 300 Longboats carried the Viking army to England.

2 As soon as they landed, the Vikings took York and seized control of much of the north of England.

Stamford Bridge

York

4 On 25 September 1066, King Harold surprised Hardrada's troops as they rested near an old bridge at Stamford. The Vikings couldn't believe that Harold had got so far north so quickly. The Battle of Stamford Bridge was about to begin!

3 King Harold's army rushed up north to meet Hardrada and Tostig. More soldiers were collected on the way to help fight the Vikings.

Normandy

Meanwhile, over in France, William waited. Fierce storms blew in the Channel, preventing his invasion boats from sailing to England.

FRANCE

What might have happened at Stamford Bridge?

1 It is early morning…

"Wake up, wake up! King Harold is here!"

2 The battle starts badly for Hardrada's men. Some have left their armour several miles away.

"Where did you leave your chain mail?"

"Near the boats… sorry!"

"I've killed 40 Englishmen with my mighty axe!"

3 However, Hardrada's men soon gain control. One brave Viking blocks the bridge so the English can't reach the Vikings.

4 With no way over the bridge, Hardrada's army fight Harold's men to a standstill. But some of Harold's men come up with a plan.

5 After an hour, King Harold's men try to stop the warrior on the bridge.

"Float under the bridge and stab him from below."

"I'll try!"

"Quick! Let's attack the Vikings while we have the chance!"

"Hurry — some have no armour."

"Arghhh!"

6 The Viking is killed and the English can get across the bridge.

"Our great King of Norway is dead!"

7 By midday King Harold's army is in control. Hardrada is killed, but the Vikings fight on.

8 Later on, Tostig is found and cut into pieces.

"Kill him!"

"Cut him up!"

"They only need 24 ships to take their battered army home to Norway!"

9 King Harold is the winner.

10 Out of respect, Harold buries his dead brother in York. But bad news arrives…

"You'll have to fight again soon, my Lord. William of Normandy has landed near Hastings."

Work

1 a What is meant by the term 'chronological order'?
b Put the following events in the correct chronological order.
- King Harold marches north to fight the Vikings.
- The two sides fight at Stamford Bridge.
- Hardrada and Tostig are killed. King Harold wins.
- The Vikings arrive in England and seize control of land in the north.
- King Harold hears that William of Normandy has landed near Hastings.

2 Write out the following statements, starting with the one that you think was most important in helping Harold win the Battle of Stamford Bridge.
- Hardrada was killed quite early in the battle.
- The Vikings were caught unprepared and without armour.
- The Viking blocking the bridge was killed.

Now, writing in full sentences and using capital letters and full stops, explain why you have put the statements in the order you have.

Harold's Housecarls
(CURRENT CHAMPIONS)

William's Knights
(THE CHALLENGERS)

DATE: 14 OCTOBER 1066
VENUE: SENLAC HILL, NEAR HASTINGS
· KICK OFF: 9.30 AM·

Mission Objectives

- Compare the weapons and tactics that were used by William's and Harold's men at the Battle of Hastings.

Hello and welcome to the town of Hastings. This is the one we've all been waiting over ten months for – the day of the battle is finally here. Here's the English line-up. It's been a tough few weeks for the English boys, despite last month's stunning victory at Stamford Bridge. The weary English have travelled 280 miles, or 450km, in nine days to meet their next opponents.

HOUSECARLS

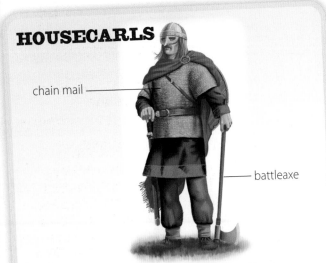

chain mail

battleaxe

KILLING POWER: 9/10

DEFENCE: 9/10

SPEED: 1/10

RANGE OF ATTACK: 1/10

The backbone of King Harold's army, there are about 2500 **housecarls** and they are well paid, fully trained and armed with the finest weapons. The favourite weapon of these bearded warriors is the huge **battleaxe**. The handle of the axe is over a metre long and its heavy blade is made of razor-sharp iron – a very precious material in 1066. A housecarl with a battleaxe is capable of chopping the head off a horse or cutting a man in half with a single blow. Their helmets, **chain mail**, large, round shields, and discipline make them excellent in defence too!

THE FYRD

javelin

sword

shield

KILLING POWER: 3/10

DEFENCE: 5/10

SPEED: 3/10

RANGE OF ATTACK: 3/10

The housecarls are supported by the **fyrd**. This mobile army isn't as experienced or well equipped as the housecarls but it's still a fierce fighting force. The leaders of the fyrd are armed with swords and **javelins** but most of their men use farming tools such as pitchforks and **scythes**. They may not be pretty, but they number over 6000 and they're fighting on their home turf!

Now let's have a look at the Normans. They've been waiting for this day ever since Harold was crowned in January and they're itching for a fight. William's **invasion** force is massive: it took over 300 ships to transport his 10,000 men and 2000 horses from France. He's even brought a fort separated into pieces with him, so he could build it here quickly! They landed at Pevensey on 28 September and soon moved to Hastings, setting fire to the town to annoy Harold.

THE ARCHERS

bow

arrows

short sword

KILLING POWER: 4/10
DEFENCE: 1/10
SPEED: 4/10
RANGE OF ATTACK: 2/10

William's 1500 archers are armed with small wooden bows that can fire six or seven arrows a minute. A skilled archer can kill a man from about 180 metres away. Archers have very little, if any, armour and are not much use when the fighting gets up close and personal!

NORMAN FOOT SOLDIERS

sword

shield

KILLING POWER: 7/10
DEFENCE: 8/10
SPEED: 2/10
RANGE OF ATTACK: 2/10

These form the main part of William's army and are armed with metre-long swords and kite-shaped shields. They attack after the enemy have been softened up by the archers' arrows and charged by the knights.

THE KNIGHTS

hauberk

spear

warhorse

KILLING POWER: 8/10
DEFENCE: 4/10
SPEED: 10/10
RANGE OF ATTACK: 8/10

William's best warriors are his 2000 knights: highly trained and fiercely loyal professional soldiers. They ride into battle on big, strong warhorses and are protected by metal helmets, chain mail suits (**hauberks**) and kite-shaped shields. Knights carry **spears** (which can be thrown or used to stab the enemy), a sword or a **mace** (a heavy metal club covered in spikes). Knights charge at full speed towards their opponents, hacking and slashing at the much slower soldiers fighting on foot beneath them.

Work

1 Match the words on the left with the correct description on the right:

Housecarl	Rides a horse into battle
Fyrd	A suit of small metal rings sewn together
Archer	Carries a battleaxe
Knight	A housecarl's main weapon
Chain mail	There are 6000 of them in Harold's army
Mace	Can fire six to seven arrows per minute
Battleaxe	A spiked club used by knights

2 a Find two ways in which William's army is better than Harold's.

   b Find two ways in which Harold's army is better than William's.

3 Which army do you think is more likely to win the battle? Give reasons and answer in full sentences.

1.6 Round 2: the Battle of Hastings – the morning

The final showdown had arrived. The Battle of Hastings would decide the future of England. King Harold had already defeated Hardrada and his Viking army and now, less than a month later, he and his army were going to have to fight all over again.

Unfortunately for Harold and his men, there had been no time to rest after winning the Battle of Stamford Bridge – they had to march 250 miles to meet William's men! So just where did the two armies face each other? Who made the first move? And which side made the best start to the battle?

Mission Objectives

- Analyse the tactics used by Harold and William in the battle.
- Judge how each of the armies fought in the early stages of the battle.

The battle begins...

Firstly, look at the picture below and read boxes 1 to 4. Then read through the cartoon on the next page to discover what happened during the first few hours of the battle.

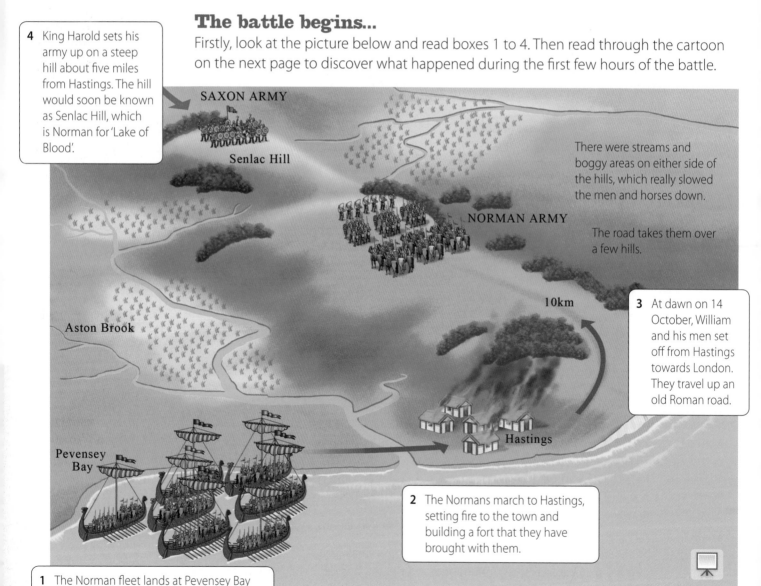

4 King Harold sets his army up on a steep hill about five miles from Hastings. The hill would soon be known as Senlac Hill, which is Norman for 'Lake of Blood'.

SAXON ARMY

Senlac Hill

There were streams and boggy areas on either side of the hills, which really slowed the men and horses down.

NORMAN ARMY

The road takes them over a few hills.

10km

Aston Brook

3 At dawn on 14 October, William and his men set off from Hastings towards London. They travel up an old Roman road.

Hastings

2 The Normans march to Hastings, setting fire to the town and building a fort that they have brought with them.

Pevensey Bay

1 The Norman fleet lands at Pevensey Bay and William's army comes ashore.

1 On 14 October, at around 9:30 in the morning, the Battle of Hastings began. William carried a flag given to him by the **Pope**. He believed this meant God was on his side. Looking up the steep hill to the English, William ordered his archers to unleash a storm of arrows.

2 Harold's men formed a tight **shield-wall** and hid behind it while the arrows fell amongst them. When the archers stopped firing, the English stood up and started banging their shields and shouting, 'Out! Out! Out!'

3 William decided to send his knights and foot soldiers to smash through the English shield-wall. Unfortunately for William, the steep hill meant his horses couldn't charge quickly. His foot soldiers were absolutely exhausted before they had even started fighting!

4 For over two hours the battle raged. The two sides stood toe-to-toe, hacking, slashing and stabbing viciously at each other. William's men just could not break through the wall of English shields that stretched across the hilltop. Then a rumour started to spread that nobody had seen William for half an hour! Had the Norman leader been killed?

5 William wasn't dead and to prove it to his men he galloped amongst them. He lifted his helmet and shouted, 'Look at me! Look at me! I am alive and, with God's help, will be the victor!'

Wise Up Words

Pope   shield-wall

Hungry for More?

Imagine you have been asked to produce a film about the Battle of Hastings. Storyboard the trailer, based on the events on these pages.

Work

1 Divide your page into two and separate the following list into factors (or reasons) that would help Harold win the battle and factors that might help William win the battle.
   - William's army had been blessed by the Pope.
   - Harold's men had just come from a battle with Hardrada.
   - The housecarls protected Harold's army with a strong shield-wall.
   - William had a large army of 10,000 men.
   - There were streams and boggy areas on both sides of Senlac Hill.

2 Write two sentences that explain why Harold placed his soldiers on the top of Senlac Hill.

3 Which side do you think is most likely to win the battle in the afternoon? Give reasons for your answer in full sentences.

Round 2: the Battle of Hastings – the afternoon

After a short break in the action, the battle started again at around 12:30pm. But neither side seemed to be winning because the same thing kept happening over and over again – the Normans kept attacking and the English kept beating away the attacks with their shield-wall! At around 3:30pm, William came up with an idea. So what was William's big plan? How was he going to get through that shield-wall? And what did this mean for King Harold?

Mission Objectives

- Evaluate how William won the Battle of Hastings.
- Discover how William went about increasing his power after the battle.

Now read through the cartoons to discover how the Battle of Hastings was finally won.

1 William had to get the English off the top of the hill. He ordered some of his soldiers to run away down the hill as if they were **retreating**. The English, thinking they were winning, charged down the hill after the Normans!

2 Without the safety of the shield-wall, Harold's men who had run down the hill were quickly cut to pieces by William's knights on horseback.

3 William saw this was his chance to win the battle – and the English crown! He hoped that if he kept repeating the trick, the English would keep falling for it. And they did! Gradually, the English shield-wall grew weaker and weaker. William then turned to his archers once more and arrows rained down on Harold's men.

4 As the sun set, Harold was killed and the battle was lost. Some said he had been shot in the eye by an arrow before being cut to pieces by some of William's men! William had the body buried at a secret location despite Harold's mother offering her son's weight in gold in exchange for the body.

After the battle

On the night of 14 October 1066, the Normans held a feast to celebrate their victory and stripped the English dead of their weapons and armour. He may have defeated Harold's army, but William didn't rule England yet. Eventually he left the battlefield and marched towards London. William made sure that every town he came across surrendered to him, while more and more soldiers sailed from Normandy to join him. By early December, William had reached London and he was crowned King of England on Christmas Day. From then on he was known as William the **Conqueror**!

The enemy within!

Although there was no danger of William being defeated by an army after Hastings, he was very nearly defeated by **dysentery**. While on the road to London, William's army was struck by agonising stomach cramps and violent diarrhoea. For some it was so bad that they had to return home to France – others died! Fortunately for William, enough remained fit to continue to London.

'Three horses were killed under him. Three times he leapt unafraid to the ground and killed the man who had killed his horse. This shows how quick he was to make his mind up and how strong he was. With savage blows of his sword, he split shields, helmets and coats of chain mail. He struck a number of enemies with his own shield. His soldiers took new courage when they saw him fighting on foot. Some, who were weak from bleeding, leant on their shields and fought on bravely. William himself helped some of his men to safety… He led his forces with great skill, holding them when they turned to run, giving them courage, sharing their danger. He was more often heard shouting to them to follow him than ordering them to go on ahead. It is clear that it was the Duke's bravery that inspired his soldiers as they went forward and gave them courage.'

▲ **SOURCE A:** *An account of William fighting in the battle, written around 1073. The man who wrote it wasn't at the battle, but based what he wrote on things he had found out.*

Work

1 Read **Source A**.
   a Write down five adjectives or phrases that *describe* William in battle.
   b Imagine you were one of William's men. Write down what you think of him.
   c Do you think the source was written by a supporter of William? Explain how you decided.
   d Can we totally trust what the source says? Explain your answer.

2 Read back through the story of the battle. Create a timeline for the battle, starting at 9:30am. Remember to include all the key events and the time they happened.

3 Why do you think the Normans stripped the English of all their weapons and armour? How could this help William control the rest of England? Answer in full sentences and use capital letters and full stops.

4 You should now know what happened at the Battle of Hastings. It's time to make up your mind – why did William win the battle? Was it:
   • because he was a brilliant and skilful leader?
   • because Harold was a poor soldier who made mistakes?
   • because the Normans were better equipped and prepared?
   • because Harold was unlucky?
   Or was it a combination of all or some of these reasons? You might want to work in groups.

Be a Top Historian

Top historians realize that different people tell different stories about the past depending on their point of view or beliefs. For example, two people would write a slightly different account of the same football match if they each supported a different side!

History Mystery

1.8 How did King Harold die?

Historians (people who study History – like you!) are like detectives who hunt for clues about people and events in history and piece them together. If they find enough evidence, a clear picture emerges and they can start to make conclusions.

Historians already know lots about the events of 1066. Some people wrote about it at the time, others told stories about what happened (which were then written down), and some people created works of art that show it.

But historians have got a problem with the death of King Harold. We definitely know he died at Hastings – he must have done because a new king began ruling England – but we just don't know *how* he died! The problem is that the sources (pieces of evidence about his death) don't all say the same thing about the way he died. So your task, as a 'History Mystery Detective', is to treat his death like a puzzle. Look through all the evidence and try to piece together how he actually died. At the end of your investigation you will have to come to your own answer to the question: 'How did King Harold die?'

Evidence A

Date 1080

Writer Amatus of Montecassino, a monk from Italy; the first written account of Harold being killed by an arrow in the eye.

'William gouged out Harold's eye with an arrow.'

Evidence B

Date 1067

Writer Guy of Amiens, a medieval writer from France

'With the point of his **lance** the first knight pierced Harold's chest, drenching the ground with blood. With his sword the second knight cut off his head. The third disembowelled him with his javelin. The fourth hacked off his leg.'

Evidence C

Date 1070

Writer William of Jumièges, a Norman monk. He claims he was at the battle. His **abbey** was given money by William the Conqueror.

'Duke William engaged the enemy at the third hour [about 9am] and continued until nightfall. Harold fell in the first shock of battle, pierced with lethal wounds.'

Evidence D

Date 1077

Made Probably made in England on the orders of Bishop Odo, King William's half-brother. Odo was at the Battle of Hastings.

This is one of the most famous pictures in British history. It is one of 72 pictures that make up a 70-metre-long piece of embroidered cloth called the Bayeux Tapestry. The scene shows two English soldiers – one with an arrow in his eye and another being cut down by a Norman on horseback. Above the picture, over both men, is written 'Hic Harold Rex Interfectus Est', which means 'Here King Harold has been killed'. But which soldier is meant to be Harold?

Wise Up Words

abbey   lance

Evidence E

Date 1130

Writer William of Malmesbury, a monk. Historians believe this source was written after he had seen the Bayeux Tapestry.

'Harold continued; but when he fell, from having his brain pierced with an arrow… he yielded to death… one of the soldiers with a sword gashed his thigh as he lay.'

Evidence F

Date 2000

Writer A modern historian.

'In recent years some people have thought that Harold might be the figure on the floor being attacked by knights, rather than the man with the arrow in his eye. But it seems obvious that the words 'Harold Rex' are written directly above the arrow-struck man. This is significant. I believe that the knights would have then attacked him.'

Evidence G

Date 1729

Artist Bernard de Montfaucon, a French monk

A fascinating image, engraved by Montfaucon after seeing a drawing of the Bayeux Tapestry in 1729. You might notice that there is no arrow in Harold's eye, but a dotted line instead. This is another mystery! Did the monk forget to draw the arrow? Or wasn't there an arrow when he saw the tapestry? Was it a lance or javelin instead? Could the arrow in the tapestry have been added on later?

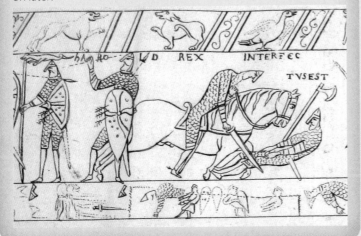

Work

To try to solve the mystery of how Harold died, start by looking closely at all the evidence on these pages.

1 **Find out all the different ways Harold may have died.**
   What weapons were used? At what stage of the battle did he die? Make a list of your findings.

2 **Find out if any of the evidence agrees on how Harold was killed.**
   Does any one piece of evidence back up what another says? Make notes on what you have found.

3 **Think – can you trust the evidence?**
   Write down why you might not trust some of the evidence. You may believe all the evidence is useful or perhaps just some of it. Do we have an English eyewitness to Harold's death? If not, why not?

4 **Now make your decision.**
   Like a detective, use evidence to back up your theory. If you're not sure, say why. In History it's OK to say you're uncertain, as long as you can explain why.

Be a Top Historian

There are some things that we just don't know about the past. Some historians say the evidence proves how Harold was killed. Others say it proves we can't be sure. Top historians will assess how **reliable** a source is, and how far we can believe it.

On the evening of 14 October 1066 (the night of the Battle of Hastings), William must have realized he was in a very dangerous position. As a foreign invader, he knew the English would want to get rid of him – soon! His army had killed the English King Harold after all, and William knew that if he gave the English time to recover they might gather another army or choose another king. So how did William deal with these problems?

Mission Objectives

- Examine William's key problems after his victory at Hastings and analyse how he dealt with them.

William's problems

William had four main problems he had to deal with. The map (**Source A**) gives details of these issues.

1 Viking threat

There is still a possibility that Vikings will invade from Norway and Denmark. If they join up with angry Englishmen in the north, they would be a very serious threat.

2 Getting to London

Anyone wishing to control England must control London. Some of Harold's army did not go with him to the Battle of Hastings; instead they stayed in London to guard it.

3 Defeating Dover

There is a fort at Dover full of tough and angry English soldiers. William must defeat these men before he marches to London or else they may attack him from behind.

4 A tired army

William's army is very tired. The Battle of Hastings was very fierce.

SOURCE A: *William's four main problems he had to deal with… quickly.*

William takes charge

William dealt with some of his problems very swiftly. **Sources B**, **C** and **D** were written or created at the time and show how determined William was to keep his new kingdom… and to show the English who was boss!

William marched to Dover where the English, stricken with fear, prepared to surrender. But our men, greedy for loot, set fire to the town. William, unwilling that those who had offered to give up, should suffer loss, gave them money for the damage his men had caused. Having captured Dover, William spent eight days making it stronger.

▲ **SOURCE B:** *Written by William of Poitiers, a friend of William's, in about 1073.*

'The Archbishop of York, the people of London and some powerful English landowners planned to put Prince Edgar [a cousin of King Edward the Confessor] on the throne. But while many were preparing to fight, the English landowners went home with their army and refused to fight William. Meanwhile, William was in the south, robbing and destroying villages in Sussex, Kent, Hampshire, Middlesex and Hertfordshire. He was even slaughtering people in these villages. William was then met by the English landowners and the leading men of London who agreed to accept him as king.'

▲ **SOURCE C:** *Florence of Worcester describes William's movements before he went to London.*

SOURCE D: *A section of the Bayeux Tapestry that shows the Normans burning an English house.*

Work

1 In your own words, explain what problems William faced immediately after the Battle of Hastings.

2 Look at **Sources B**, **C** and **D**.
   a Why do you think William was kind to the English in Dover but so cruel as he marched towards London?
   b In what way is **Source C** similar to **Source D**?

3 What problems has William not yet dealt with? You may want to re-read **Source A** (the map) to help you here.

The march to London

William took two months to reach London, and on the way his army burned, stole and killed anything it passed. In December, the English soldiers in London gave in and William entered the city. He was crowned King of England in Westminster Abbey on Christmas Day 1066 (see **Source A**).

But the new king still had to conquer the rest of England. And the people in the north of England, helped by Vikings from Denmark, weren't giving up easily. When William's trusted friend, Earl Robert, and 900 of William's soldiers were murdered when they were sent up to rule Durham, the king acted quickly – and brutally – to deal with the rebels. **Sources B**, **C** and **D** show just how tough the new king was.

SOURCE A: *William is crowned King of England, as shown in a medieval manuscript.*

SOURCE B: *There is rebellion in the north, as told in the Anglo-Saxon Chronicle.* Prince Edgar was a cousin of Edward the Confessor and many people thought he was the rightful king of England!

'William gave Northumberland to Earl Robert [his friend] but the people of Durham **massacred** Robert and 900 of his soldiers. Prince Edgar and the rebels came to York and the people of the city joined them. William came from the south and suprised them, ravaging York and killing hundreds… Then Vikings came from Denmark with 240 ships and joined up with the English. With a huge and joyful army they stormed York and killed hundreds of William's men, burned the castle and captured lots of treasure.'

SOURCE C: *William's revenge, known as the 'Harrying of the North', was brutal, as this medieval account shows. Some estimate that 100,000 people died from starvation after William's troops had destroyed all the animals and crops.* ▼

'William came to York but learned that the Vikings had fled. He ordered his men to repair the castle. He set out to search the forests and remote mountains, stopping at nothing to hunt down the rebels hidden there. He cut down many and destroyed and burned homes. Nowhere else had William shown such cruelty. His fury was blind and he punished the innocent with the guilty. He ordered that all crops, cattle and food be burned, so that the whole region had nothing to live on.'

'I fell on the Northen shires like a hungry lion. I ordered their houses and corn with all their tools and goods to be burned and great herds of cattle to be butchered. I took my revenge by giving them famine. Alas I kept the throne by so many crimes.'

▲ **SOURCE D:** *King William's deathbed confession, written by Orderic Vitalis in about 1130. Orderic wasn't there at the time and has given his own version of what William said.*

William shows his power

Although William had dealt with his problems he ordered that his loyal friends who would help him run England to build strong fortresses, called castles, to protect themselves.

King William's men built castles all over England. **Source E** shows the extent of his castle-making plans in the years after Hastings. He brought over dozens and dozens of his most loyal friends from Normandy to live in them. By 1071, five years after he had won the Battle of Hastings, King William was master of England – William the Conqueror. His next challenge was to stay in charge!

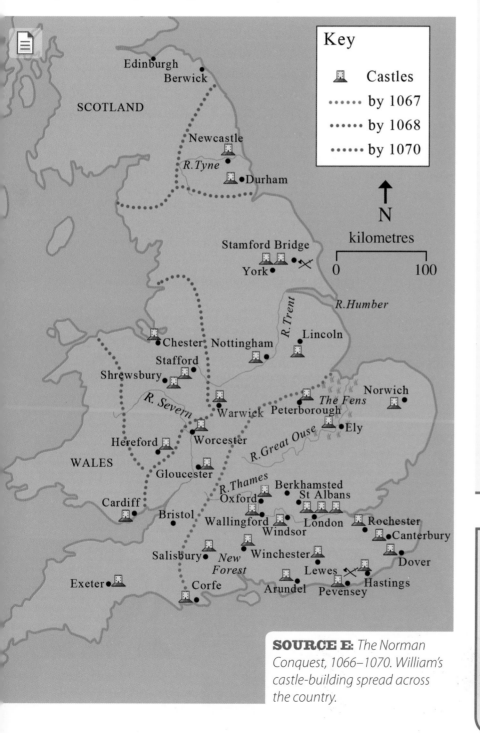

SOURCE E: *The Norman Conquest, 1066–1070. William's castle-building spread across the country.*

Wise Up Words

massacred

Work

1 The way King William crushed the people in the north of England is known as the 'Harrying of the North'. Copy and complete the following table. You will find the information in the text and sources on pages 32 to 35.

The Harrying of the North 1069–1070	
What caused the people of the north to rebel?	
What did the English rebels actually do?	
What did William do?	

2 a What is meant by the word 'famine'?
  b How did William use famine as a weapon?
  c What are the advantages and disadvantages of William's actions?

3 Historians have said that William punished the people in the north to teach the whole country a lesson. What do you think this means?

4 a What is a castle?
  b Why did William instruct his friends who were helping him run the country to build castles?

Hungry for More?

 The Big Write!

Work with a partner. One of you should write a letter to William, as if you were an English earl, complaining about the way he is treating the English. The other person should write back as William, explaining why you are being so brutal.

William the castle-builder

To the English, King William was a foreigner. He was a Frenchman, who spoke French and had French friends. Most Englishmen hated him and wanted him dead! But after about five years as king, William had managed to put down all the rebellions against his rule. He now had to think about the long-term future. How could he stay in control of England?

Mission Objectives

- Understand what is meant by a 'motte and bailey' castle.
- Assess the advantages and disadvantages of these castles.

William builds castles

William brought his rich and powerful friends over from Normandy to help control the English. In return for this support he gave them large areas of English land. These friends became powerful landowners known as barons. They soon realized that they needed protection from attacks by unhappy Englishmen. So they decided to build castles. **Source A** shows the sort of castles that William's barons built. By 1086, over 100 castles had been built across England (see **Source B**).

Reduced to rubble

These new buildings were known as **motte and bailey** castles. They had to be built quickly and wherever the Normans wanted them. If some houses or a village stood where the baron wanted a castle, he simply built on top of them. In Cambridge 25 houses were pulled down to make way for a new castle. In Lincoln the Normans pulled down over 150 houses.

Norman barons and their soldiers used motte and bailey castles as a base from which to control the local area. They were built at key points, to guard important roads, ports, river crossings, and towns. They became the focus for local trade in the area, which the baron could then tax.

But the problem with castles that go up quickly is that they can be brought down just as fast. Wooden fences and buildings can burn, be smashed down, or rot. So, by as early as 1070, any barons with a bit of time and money began to build their castles in stone instead.

SOURCE A: *A motte and bailey castle. Each one took 7 to14 days to build.*

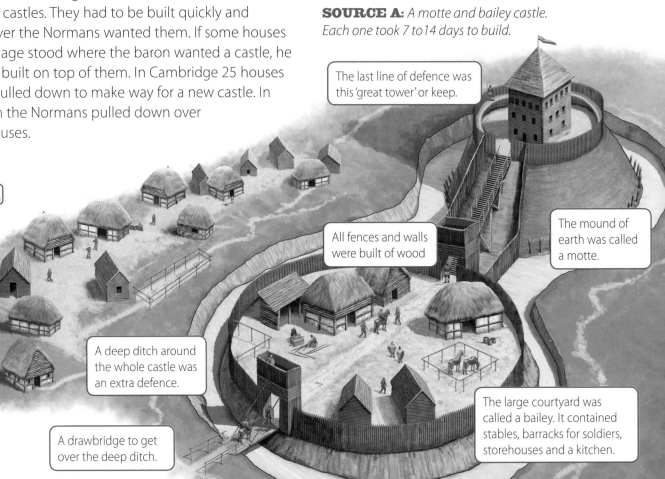

The last line of defence was this 'great tower' or keep.

All fences and walls were built of wood

The mound of earth was called a motte.

A deep ditch around the whole castle was an extra defence.

The large courtyard was called a bailey. It contained stables, barracks for soldiers, storehouses and a kitchen.

A drawbridge to get over the deep ditch.

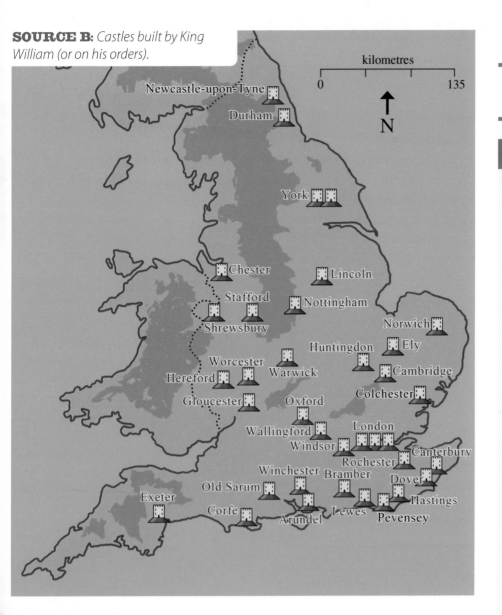

SOURCE B: *Castles built by King William (or on his orders).*

kilometres

0   135

N

Newcastle-upon-Tyne
Durham
York
Chester   Lincoln
Stafford   Nottingham
Shrewsbury
Norwich
Huntingdon   Ely
Worcester   Warwick   Cambridge
Hereford
Gloucester   Oxford   Colchester
Wallingford   London
Windsor   Canterbury
Rochester
Winchester   Bramber   Dover
Old Sarum   Hastings
Exeter   Corfe   Lewes
Arundel   Pevensey

SOURCE C: *One of the world's most famous castles, the Tower of London was once the home of King William. It was originally built out of wood and later replaced with stone. The Tower of London was the first stone keep in England.*

Work

1 There are ten words missing from the paragraph below. Copy out the paragraph and fill in the missing words from the list underneath it.

Although _____ was now _____ of England, he still had the problem of controlling the defeated _____ . So he brought over his _____ and powerful friends from _____ in France to help him do this. He gave them large areas of _____ and asked them to _____ them on his behalf. These _____ , as they were called, built large fortresses known as _____ and _____ castles to live in while they ruled their land.

barons   motte   Normandy
King   William   rich   English
land   bailey   control

2 Why do you think the keep was built on a high mound of earth? What advantages would the height give to those in the keep?

3  **The Big Write!**

Imagine you are an angry Englishman who has just led a failed attack on a motte and bailey castle. Describe the obstacles you faced on the way to the keep before you were finally defeated. Remember to include what you think were the weaknesses of the wooden castle.

The Domesday Book

Most of us know how much money we've got. We usually know roughly how much is in our pockets or our bank accounts. We know what we own and are usually interested in what other people own too. William the Conqueror was exactly the same – he was keen to know all about the country he had conquered and how much it was worth. In 1085 he decided to find out.

Mission Objectives

- Explain the purpose of the Domesday Survey and the Domesday Book.

The survey

William sent officials all over England to visit every village and ask a series of detailed questions. They interviewed the priest, the steward (the man who organized the farm work in the village) and six elderly villagers in each village.

The officials took a year to visit over 13,000 villages. Soldiers who travelled with them threatened to kill people if they didn't tell the truth. A second group visited the villages later to check the people had been honest!

Why do you think that the officials wanted to interview the priest? Why do you think they wanted to talk to the elderly villagers too?

Hungry for More?

'[The official] made them search so thoroughly that there was not a single yard of land, nor even – it is a shame to tell it but he was not ashamed to do it – one ox, nor a cow, nor a swine that was not set down in his writing.'

▲ **SOURCE A:** *A monk describes the thoroughness of the officials.*

How much farmland is there?

Who owned this land before William was king?

How many pigs are there?

How much woodland is there?

How much is the land worth?

How many people live here?

How many fishponds?

How many cows?

How many mills are there?

The book

All the records from the village surveys were sent to Winchester where one man wrote it all down in Latin. The surveys filled two huge books and contained approximately two million words.

The book gave William knowledge, and knowledge was a powerful thing. It meant:

- he could work out how much each person in England could afford to pay him in taxes
- he knew exactly how many people he could get to fight for him
- he could settle any quarrels over who owned which bit of land.

However, William never got to see the finished book. While riding his horse in 1087, he slipped forward in his saddle and burst open his bladder. He died in agony. He wouldn't have been able to read it himself anyway – he couldn't read!

> 'At Lincoln, 116 houses were destroyed to make way for the castle.'

▲ **SOURCE B:** *An English translation of a section of the Domesday Book.*

> 'Richard holds Birmingham from William. There is land for 6 ploughs, there is one plough in the demesne [lord's land]. There are 5 villeins and 4 bordars and 2 ploughs. There is a wood half a mile long and 4 furlongs broad. In the time of King Edward it was worth 20 shillings and it is still worth the same.'

▲ **SOURCE C:** *Another extract from the Domesday Book. Birmingham is now the second largest city in England. A furlong is about 200 metres. Villeins and bordars were people who lived on and farmed the Lord's land.*

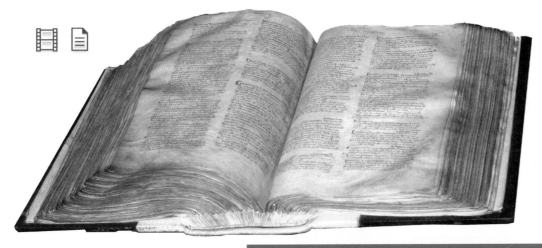

SOURCE D: *The Domesday Book still survives today. It is kept in the National Archives in London.*

Work

1 **a** Explain why the Domesday Book was made.
   b Why did it become known as the Domesday Book?

2 Read **Source A**.
   a What idea does it give us about what the survey was like for villagers?
   b Do you think the monk was happy about King William's survey or not? Explain your answer. Include any clues that might tell us how the monk felt.

3 Read **Source B**. What does the source tell us about King William's attitude towards the English?

4 According to **Sources A** and **B**, what kind of man was William?

5 Read **Source C**. In your own words, write a paragraph describing Birmingham in 1086.

The feudal system: who's the boss?

Wherever we go, wherever we've been, there's usually someone in control – at home, in the classroom, at work or at a youth club. The person in charge might be a parent, a teacher or a manager. None of us lives in a world where we can do what we want when we want to. Knowing this makes the next two pages very straightforward. By the end you'll understand exactly how King William controlled England.

Mission Objectives

- Examine the feudal system and be able to illustrate exactly how it worked.

Clever William

King William said that all the land in England belonged to him. But England was too large for him to manage by himself, so how did he stay in charge? His answer was to use a system of sharing out the land. The king still owned it, of course, but he could lend large areas of land to people in return for their **loyalty**.

Most of the people he lent the land to had helped him in the Battle of Hastings. He was rewarding them for helping him. 'Feudal' is the Latin word for 'land', so because the new system was based on land, it became known as the **feudal system**. The diagram on this page illustrates how William's system worked.

FACT!

King William didn't give his barons one large area of land – he carefully gave them several pieces dotted around England. He did this to make it difficult for the barons to build up large armies in the same area. If they became too powerful, he feared they might rebel against him.

The king

lends land to

pay for the land, and provide knights for the king

The barons (about 200 in total)

lend land to

pay for the land and fight for barons if needed

The knights (about 4000 in total)

lend land to

pay for the land in work and food

The villeins (about 1.5 million in total)

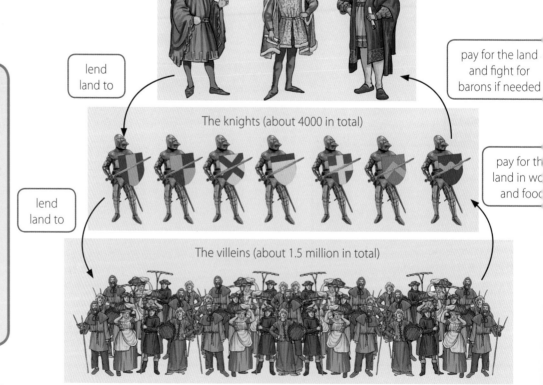

How did William control his kingdom?

King William's idea was very clever. He knew he needed help running England, so he used all the land he owned as a way of getting assistance. By giving lots of land to his friends (the barons), he got their support and help… and some money when he taxed them.

But how did the barons get their money? Simple! By giving away some of their land to knights (very well-trained soldiers) who then paid taxes to the barons. The knights were very loyal to the barons because if they weren't, the barons could take their land away!

In turn, the knights shared much of their land with the peasants (known as **villeins**) who then farmed the land and paid taxes to the knights. In this way, nearly every man in the country got some land – but he had to promise to be loyal to the man who gave it to him. If he broke his promise, he lost his land.

So this very clever system meant that William had a constant supply of money rolling in from his barons (who got it from the knights who got it from the peasants)… and he *still* managed to own all the land! Even though most of the land was being used by other people, nearly everyone was loyal to him.

SOURCE A: *A baron swearing an 'oath of loyalty' to the king. This means he is promising to be loyal to the king and never betray him.*

FACT!

In the Middle Ages, a 'lord' was anyone above you in the feudal system. So a peasant had several lords, while a baron had just one – the king!

'I become your man from this day forward, for life and limb and loyalty. I shall be true and faithful to you for the lands I hold from you.'

▲ **SOURCE B:** *An oath which a baron made to the king when he was given land.*

Wise Up Words

feudal system   loyalty   villein

Work

1 a Copy out the following statements and match each statement to the right person.
- I give land to the knights who pay me taxes and fight for me when required.
- I am at the bottom of the pile. Everyone is my lord!
- I own all the land.
- The peasants are loyal to me, but I am loyal to the baron… and the king, of course!

    | King | | Baron | | Knight | | Peasant |

b Now write out the four people again, but this time, make up your own comment for each one.

2 a How did the feudal system make it easier for King William to control the English?

b Why was William careful not to give his barons pieces of land that were close together?

3 Look at **Source A**.
a Which man is the king? Give reasons for why you think this.
b What is happening in the picture?

4 Look at **Source B**.
a Write a sentence to summarize what the baron is promising the king.
b These promises were sometimes made in the presence of a priest or near a Bible. Why do you think this was?

The earliest castles were built of wood – and were built very quickly. They were intended to keep out enemies and to keep people, horses and treasures safe. They dominated river crossings, roadways and towns and were used as a base from which the baron could control the local population. So how and why did castle-building change?

Mission Objectives

- Investigate how and why castles changed after 1066.

The early wooden castles, which were built by King William and his followers after their victory at the Battle of Hastings, were good at reminding the English people that they had been beaten – but they were very weak against a determined attack. The wooden walls could quite easily be chopped or burnt down, or just climbed over with ladders. So as early as 1070, a few lords with the time, money and a suitable location began to build their castles in stone (see **Source A**).

The wooden tower was knocked down and a stone keep built instead. It was much larger than the wooden one and contained most of the castle's important rooms – the lord's personal rooms, the kitchen, chapel, main hall, stores, guardroom, and dungeon.

The wooden fence was pulled down and a tall stone one built in its place. This was called a **curtain wall**.

The curtain wall was often wide enough for soldiers to walk along the top.

A wide, deep ditch called a moat made it very difficult for attackers to get close to the castle walls. If they tried to tunnel under the walls, the tunnel would fill with water.

Battlements provided a barrier for soldiers to hide behind when they fired arrows.

A well-guarded drawbridge.

SOURCE A: *An early stone castle. The massive square keep towered over the countryside, striking fear or respect into the hearts of those who saw it.*

Be a Top Historian

A key history skill is being able to spot **change and continuity**. This means that during the period you are studying there will be things that **change** and some things that stay the same (**continue**). Look out for change and continuity when looking at the story of castles from 1066 to the 1400s.

If a castle's outer walls were really strong, sometimes the lord didn't even bother with the keep at all. They were dark, noisy, smoky places anyway, and lacked privacy, so sometimes a lord would build all the rooms, buildings and accommodation he needed within the bailey itself. He would then strengthen the curtain wall with extra towers and build an especially tough entrance called a **barbican** or gatehouse (see **Sources B** and **C**).

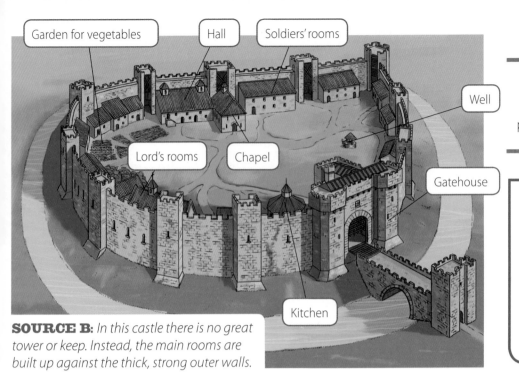

Garden for vegetables · Hall · Soldiers' rooms · Well · Lord's rooms · Chapel · Gatehouse · Kitchen

SOURCE B: *In this castle there is no great tower or keep. Instead, the main rooms are built up against the thick, strong outer walls.*

Wise Up Words

barbican battlements
concentric castle curtain wall
portcullis trebuchet undermine

What Happened When? 1070

In 1070, William the Conqueror started building Windsor Castle, which today is an official residence of the Queen. It is the oldest and largest inhabited castle in the world.

Defending soldiers · Hot water · Two wall towers, containing guardrooms for the soldiers · Murder holes · **Portcullis** (gate) made from iron · Attackers

SOURCE C: *A gatehouse or barbican.*

FACT!

Being able to defend a castle was a top priority and any attackers who made it through the portcullis faced tough resistance! Defending soldiers would sometimes pour boiling water, tar or lead down holes in the roof of the barbican known as 'murder holes'. Heavy stones could also be dropped onto attackers, while archers shot arrows at intruders through slits in the wall!

Work

1 Look at the five statements below. Three are correct, whilst two have mistakes in them. Copy out all five sentences, making sure you correct the two that are wrong.
   - The first Norman castles were built on King William's orders.
   - The earliest castles were built of stone.
   - A motte was a deep ditch that surrounded a castle.
   - The stone wall built around a castle was called a curtain wall.
   - After 1070, some wooden castles were replaced with stone ones.

2 Match up the features in **List A** with the correct definitions from **List B**.

List A	List B
• Motte	• A wall with gaps along the top for firing through
• Bailey	• The strongest and tallest place in the castle
• Keep	• A deep ditch around the castle
• Moat	• An extra-strong gatehouse
• Barbican	• A courtyard in which the buildings stood
• Portcullis	• A mound of earth upon which the keep was built
• Battlement	• A tough iron gate

Mission impossible

In the early 1200s, things seemed impossible for the attacker. The castle walls were so thick (sometimes five metres thick) and so well defended that breaking through them would have taken forever. And if, by some miracle, an attacking army got through the wall and saw a huge stone keep in front of them, it was usually too high to climb up and the defenders would be up there fighting back.

Attack!

However, it didn't take long before attackers came up with new ideas that would change the shape of castles. It was discovered that the square corners of the towers and the keep were weak and could be **undermined**. This meant they collapsed if attackers dug tunnels underneath them. Also, better and better machines (such as massive catapults called **trebuchets**) were being designed that could throw huge boulders at the walls and batter them. So the defenders had to come up with new ideas to protect themselves and developed the **concentric castle**!

Clever castles

The concentric castle was an idea brought back by the knights fighting abroad in the Holy Land around Jerusalem. They were more regular in shape than earlier castles and used water defences wherever possible. This made it harder for attackers to get their catapults near the walls. The towers were round, so they were harder to undermine by digging underneath them, and each set of walls decreased in height so that archers on the upper walls could shoot over the heads of the soldiers below (see **Sources A**, **B**, and **C**).

SOURCE A: *A concentric castle. This drawing is based on the design of a real castle – Beaumaris Castle in Anglesey, Wales.*

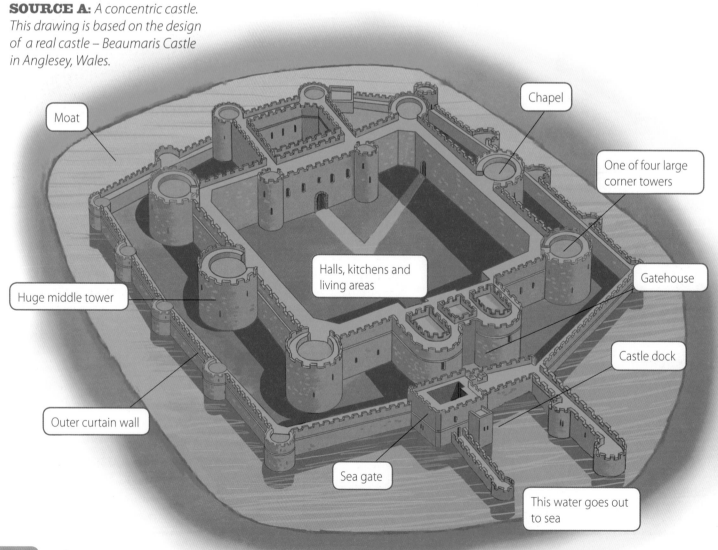

Moat

Chapel

One of four large corner towers

Huge middle tower

Halls, kitchens and living areas

Gatehouse

Outer curtain wall

Castle dock

Sea gate

This water goes out to sea

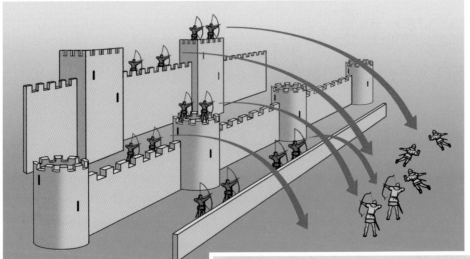

SOURCE B: *How walls of different heights helped the defenders. The enemy can be fired on from three different levels.*

Comfier castles

The great age of castle-building began to decline in the early 1400s. The country became more peaceful and there was no need for such strong, expensive castles to be built. Instead, they were changed and modified to become lavish homes, and new ones were built for comfort first and defence second (see **Source D**).

SOURCE C: *Caerphilly Castle in Wales is an example of a concentric castle.*

SOURCE D: *A picture of Herstmonceux Castle in East Sussex. After 1400, most castles were no longer heavily fortified. This one had brick walls and large windows.*

EITHER: Design a leaflet, poster or mind-map that explains and illustrates how castles have changed from 1066 to the 1400s.

Interview with…

OR: Work with a friend or partner (or on your own, if you wish) to come up with a series of questions to ask one of the medieval world's most famous concentric castle designers – James of St George. This person really existed and designed several of Britain's most famous castles including Conwy, Harlech and Beaumaris (see **Source A**). You want to impress him with your interview skills and historical knowledge, so come up with some really interesting questions. Then, write down the answers he might have given.

The Big Write!

OR: Write an extended answer or essay. The title is: 'How and why did castles change between 1066 and the 1400s?' Remember to plan and draft your essay and keep in mind that all good essays need an introduction and a conclusion!

The siege of Rochester Castle

In 1215, a group of rebel barons weren't happy with their king, John, because they felt he was a poor leader. To make matters worse, he kept asking the barons for more and more money in taxes to pay for his unsuccessful wars.

Rochester Castle in Kent was very important to King John because it guarded one of the main roads in and out of London. The barons knew this, so they seized control in the summer of 1215. So what did John do when he found out? How did he try to get his castle back? And how did 40 fat pigs come to the king's rescue?

Mission Objectives

- Recall the names of at least five weapons, methods or tactics used to get into a castle.
- Summarize how each of these weapons, methods or tactics was designed to work.
- Explain in detail how King John eventually got into Rochester Castle.

The siege begins

Rochester Castle was very well defended. In 1206, King John himself had spent a fortune improving the castle's ditches and keep – making it one of the strongest castles in the country! The outer walls were over three metres thick and the walls of the main tower were over 34 metres high. So at first, the king decided to lay **siege** to the castle. From the French word 'siéger', meaning 'to sit', a siege is when attackers literally 'sit' down and wait. They stop anyone getting in or out of the castle – and when the food runs out, the people inside have to give up and surrender, or starve to death.

However, after a few weeks the king realized that he was wasting his time. The barons had enough food and water to hold out for weeks, maybe months. So the king scrapped the siege and instructed his army to use some of the latest weapons – **battering rams**, **mangonels** and **trebuchets** – to get in and defeat the rebellious barons. Look carefully at the cartoon on the next page. It shows some of the key weapons King John used to try and get into Rochester Castle.

SOURCE A: *Rochester Castle, in Kent, was one of the most important and best defended castles in England at the time.*

FACT!

King John lost so many battles in France that he was nicknamed 'Softsword'. He even lost Normandy, the birthplace of William the Conqueror!

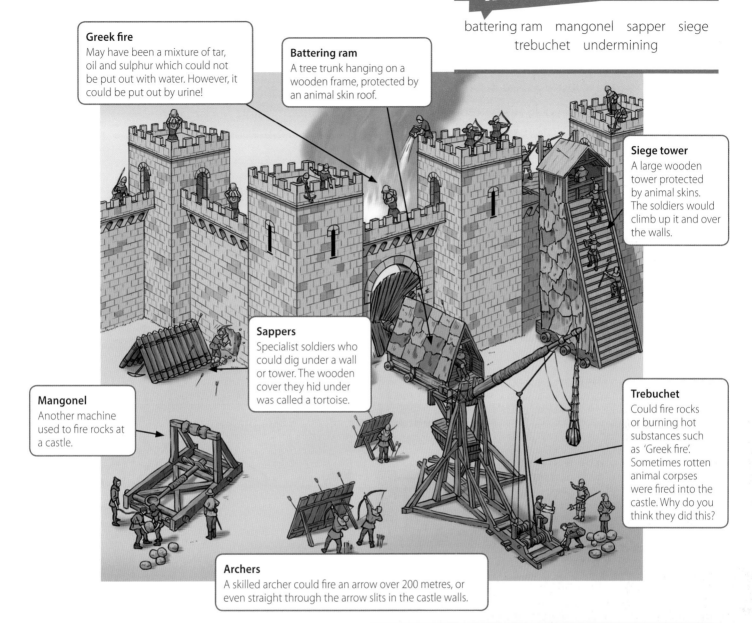

Greek fire
May have been a mixture of tar, oil and sulphur which could not be put out with water. However, it could be put out by urine!

Battering ram
A tree trunk hanging on a wooden frame, protected by an animal skin roof.

Siege tower
A large wooden tower protected by animal skins. The soldiers would climb up it and over the walls.

Sappers
Specialist soldiers who could dig under a wall or tower. The wooden cover they hid under was called a tortoise.

Mangonel
Another machine used to fire rocks at a castle.

Trebuchet
Could fire rocks or burning hot substances such as 'Greek fire'. Sometimes rotten animal corpses were fired into the castle. Why do you think they did this?

Archers
A skilled archer could fire an arrow over 200 metres, or even straight through the arrow slits in the castle walls.

But as hard as they tried, King John's soldiers just couldn't smash down all of the castle's thick walls and get to the barons. After a few weeks, things were getting desperate for the king; he received news that another group of rebels were about to come and help the ones trapped inside the castle, so he needed another plan… and quickly!

King John had been falling out with his barons for most of his reign. Why not try to find out more about their quarrels? TOP TIP: You might want to start your research with something called 'Magna Carta'.

Hungry for More?

Work

1 a Why did the barons inside Rochester Castle rebel against King John?
   b Why was Rochester Castle so important to both the rebels **and** King John? Give reasons for your answer.

2 Match up the weapons and tactics in **List A** with their correct definitions from **List B**.

List A	List B
• Siege	• A huge catapult
• Trebuchet	• A covered ladder
• Battering ram	• From the French for 'to sit'
• Siege tower	• A special mixture that's set on fire
• Greek fire	• Swings at doors and walls to make a hole

Dig, dig, dig!

By the beginning of November, after trying to regain the castle for several weeks, King John had achieved *some* success… but not much! His battering rams and trebuchets had managed to break down some of the outer walls, but he still couldn't get to the barons who were inside the great stone keep, protected by walls over three metres thick. So John decided on a new tactic, known as **undermining**.

Undermining was when a group of miners (called **sappers**) would dig a tunnel under a castle wall or the corner of a castle's tower and hollow out a huge cavern underneath. They would prop up the roof of their cavern with wooden supports. Then, when they felt the cavern was big enough, the wooden supports would be burned so that it would collapse… and bring everything above down with it. **Source A** shows you how undermining worked.

Hungry for More?

King John was the great-, great-grandson of William the Conqueror, the famous winner of the Battle of Hastings. After William's death in 1087, both of his sons became king, then his grandson, great-grandson… and then two great-, great-grandsons. There was a female ruler too, for a while, although she was never officially crowned queen. She was William's granddaughter. Why not find out all of their names?

SOURCE A: *How undermining worked.*

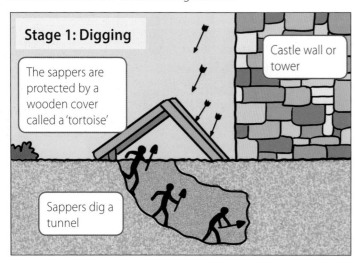

Stage 1: Digging

The sappers are protected by a wooden cover called a 'tortoise'

Castle wall or tower

Sappers dig a tunnel

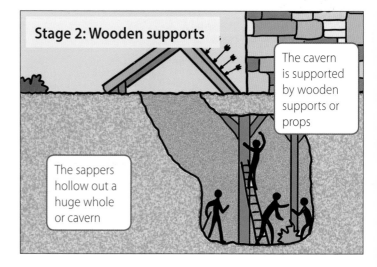

Stage 2: Wooden supports

The cavern is supported by wooden supports or props

The sappers hollow out a huge whole or cavern

Stage 3: Fire

A soldier with a flaming torch enters the cavern

The wooden supports are set on fire

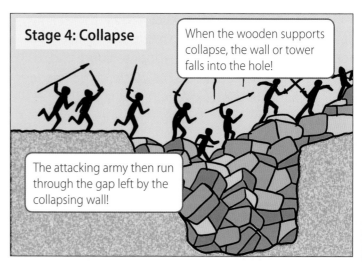

Stage 4: Collapse

When the wooden supports collapse, the wall or tower falls into the hole!

The attacking army then run through the gap left by the collapsing wall!

Feeling the heat

Undermining a castle's walls was a clever tactic, but it didn't always work! Sometimes the wooden supports didn't burn through properly and the walls didn't fall all the way down into the hole. So King John decided to make sure the fire in the underground cavern was very, very hot, to be certain that the wooden supports would be totally destroyed… so he sent for some extra fat pigs! (See **Source B**).

Pig power!

As soon as the pigs arrived, John knew he'd have the walls of the keep down in no time. Pig fat burns at a very, very high temperature (up to around 500°C), so John piled up the pigs in the huge cavern dug deep below the castle walls… and set them on fire! The fat burned so well that the wooden supports collapsed, the cavern caved in and the foundations of the wall above began to crack. Eventually, the wall of the keep fell down and the whole south-east tower fell into the hole. It was then that the king stormed in. On 30 November 1215, the siege of Rochester Castle was finally over – thanks to 40 fat pigs!

FACT!

King John didn't punish the rebel barons as severely as many thought he would. He needed their money, after all, and decided it would be best if they were kept alive so that he could tax them heavily. However, he did get his revenge on one man who changed sides halfway through the siege and joined the rebels. What did King John do to the unfortunate man? He ordered his hands and feet to be cut off!

> *'Send to us with all speed by day and night, forty of the fattest pigs of the sort least good for eating so that we may bring fire underneath the castle.'*

▲ **SOURCE B:** *King John's order to find 40 fat pigs. This has to be one of the strangest royal requests ever!*

SOURCE C: *This picture from a medieval manuscript shows a king (probably John) out hunting with his dogs.*

Work

1. ✎ In your own words, explain how King John finally managed to get into Rochester Castle. In your answer, you MUST use the following terms: sappers; undermining; wooden supports; pig fat.

2. Now you have read about the siege of Rochester Castle, it's time to put your knowledge about attacking and defending castles into practice.
   The year is 1304 and Stirling Castle is under siege! In pairs, consider the sort of events that might have taken place during the final week of the siege.

   a. One person takes the role of the attacker. Think about what tricks and weapons you could use to get in. The other person takes the role of the baron, defending his castle. Think about what defences you have for keeping the attackers out.

   b. In pairs, discuss the events that might occur during this last week.

   c. ✎ Write a siege diary from the point of view of your character. Include all the events of that week. How the siege ends is up to you.

A castle was very busy because it was a lord or baron's home – it was full of people who looked after him, such as servants, cooks and entertainers. But it was also a local centre of government used as a base from which the lord or baron ruled the local area. On behalf of the king, a lord or baron would be expected to collect taxes, arrest criminals, prevent rebellion, and guard against invasion, and lots of different people were needed to do this.

A castle was rather like a town hall and a police station all rolled into one, and was always full of people busily going about their business. So who were the castle's most important and interesting inhabitants?

Mission Objectives

- Examine what day-to-day life in a castle was like and know the names and jobs of the people who lived there.

I am the **baron**. I own the castle and all the land around it. I even own the peasants working on my land. I have other castles in different parts of the country too. I spend my money on fantastic food, beautiful wall hangings, gold and silver jewellery, and entertaining my friends.

I am the **baron's wife**, one of the few women who live in the castle. I look after our children, with help from my personal servants known as ladies-in-waiting. I can sew, sing and play musical instruments, so I can impress my husband's important friends when they come and visit.

As the **steward**, I am responsible for all the servants — the cooks, butlers, serving staff, gardeners, and even the gong farmer!

I stink. I'm the **gong farmer**, that's why! My job is to clean out all the **garderobes** or toilets.

I am the **constable** and my main focus is security. The safety of the castle is my responsibility so I make sure the soldiers control who or what comes in and out of this place. I actually run the whole castle when the lord is away.

I am the **marshall**. I look after the horses and carts, the blacksmiths, stonemasons, and carpenters.

I am the **chamberlain**. I look after my lord and lady's rooms and all their belongings. I also look after their clothes and make sure the servants clean them properly. I am trusted to look after all my lord's money and valuables. I make sure good accounts are kept of all the taxes paid and every penny spent.

I am a **forgotten prisoner** in the **oubliette** and have stolen from the baron. I am on display as a warning to others. My body will stay here for months. Birds and maggots will eat my flesh until only bones are left.

There is so much work to be done around here and we are too busy to stop and explain exactly what we do. As **servants**, we are the ones who cook, clean, wash, serve, tidy, fetch, and carry. Few of us even have proper rooms, so we just sleep anywhere we can.

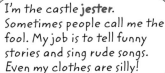

I'm the castle **jester**. Sometimes people call me the fool. My job is to tell funny stories and sing rude songs. Even my clothes are silly!

My job as a **sheriff** is to arrest criminals, collect taxes and make sure people keep the laws. I don't live in the castle, but visit it often to meet with the lord.

I've got 21 days to go! As a **knight**, my main job is to protect my lord. I do this for 40 days a year because the baron gave me some land. I use men who live on my land as soldiers to help me. When my 40 days are over another knight who lives nearby will come and do his duty.

We work for him! Our job as **soldiers** is to defend the castle and protect the baron when he travels around.

Wise Up Words

garderobe   oubliette

Work

1 a Make a copy of the puzzle template and fill it in using clues 1 to 5.

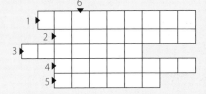

CLUES:
1 Forgotten prisoner
2 Looks after horses and carts
3 Arrests criminals
4 Defenders of the castle
5 Works for the baron for 40 days

b Now read *down* the grid (clue 6) and write a sentence or two about this person.

2 Choose one of the characters from the castle. Imagine that they have fallen from the battlements by accident! It's your job to recruit someone to fill their post. Write a job advert to find a replacement. Remember to include a full job description and the skills required for this post.

Who's the king of the castle?

Part of the reason for building a castle was to create an impression. The baron wanted to show everyone that he was in charge, and that he was there to stay! Imagine how impressive and powerful a castle must have looked 800 years ago when it was new. It would have been the tallest building anyone had ever seen, and the huge towers and high stone walls would have been topped with menacing soldiers staring out over the towns, villages and fields below.

The castle was also a safe base from which the baron or lord could rule the local area. There was no fixed plan or shape for a castle, so each one was different depending on how the baron wanted it constructed. This is why all castles look a little bit different.

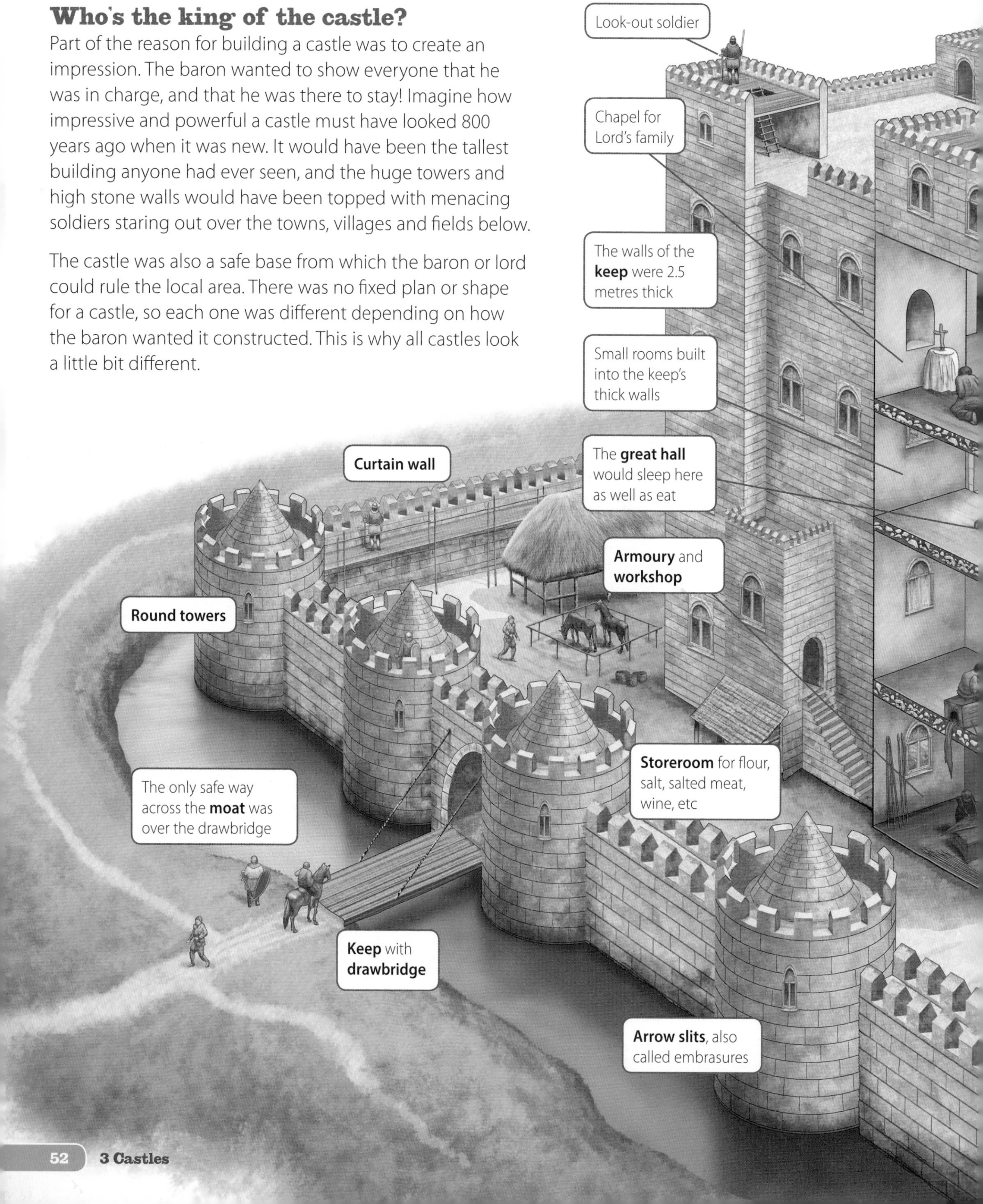

Look-out soldier

Chapel for Lord's family

The walls of the **keep** were 2.5 metres thick

Small rooms built into the keep's thick walls

Curtain wall

The **great hall** would sleep here as well as eat

Round towers

Armoury and **workshop**

Storeroom for flour, salt, salted meat, wine, etc

The only safe way across the **moat** was over the drawbridge

Keep with **drawbridge**

Arrow slits, also called embrasures

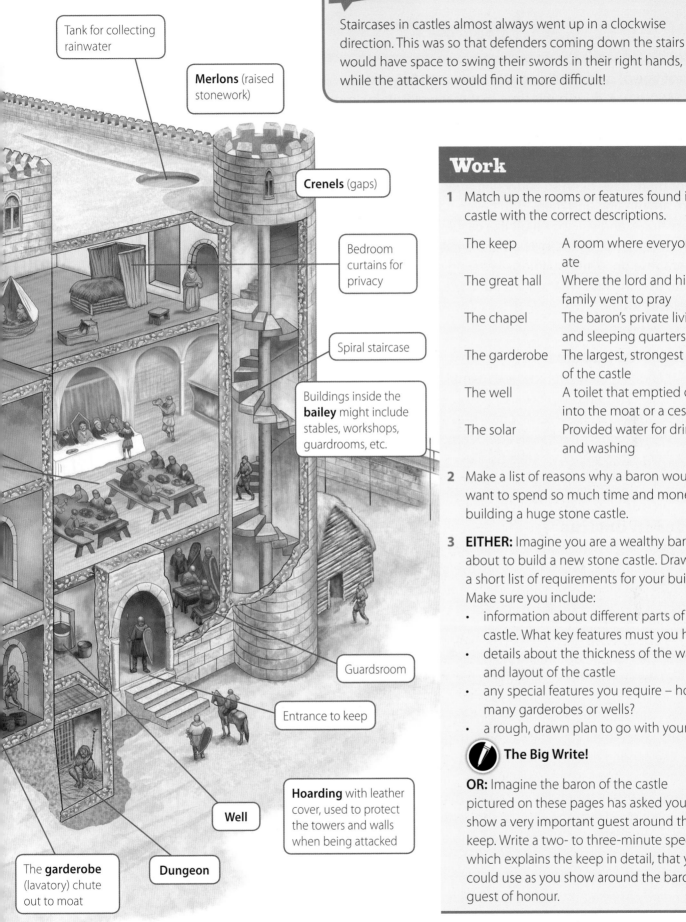

Tank for collecting rainwater

Merlons (raised stonework)

Crenels (gaps)

Bedroom curtains for privacy

Spiral staircase

Buildings inside the **bailey** might include stables, workshops, guardrooms, etc.

Guardsroom

Entrance to keep

Hoarding with leather cover, used to protect the towers and walls when being attacked

Well

Dungeon

The **garderobe** (lavatory) chute out to moat

Staircases in castles almost always went up in a clockwise direction. This was so that defenders coming down the stairs would have space to swing their swords in their right hands, while the attackers would find it more difficult!

Work

1 Match up the rooms or features found in a castle with the correct descriptions.

The keep	A room where everyone ate
The great hall	Where the lord and his family went to pray
The chapel	The baron's private living and sleeping quarters
The garderobe	The largest, strongest part of the castle
The well	A toilet that emptied out into the moat or a cesspool
The solar	Provided water for drinking and washing

2 Make a list of reasons why a baron would want to spend so much time and money building a huge stone castle.

3 **EITHER:** Imagine you are a wealthy baron about to build a new stone castle. Draw up a short list of requirements for your builder. Make sure you include:
   - information about different parts of the castle. What key features must you have?
   - details about the thickness of the walls and layout of the castle
   - any special features you require – how many garderobes or wells?
   - a rough, drawn plan to go with your list.

    The Big Write!

OR: Imagine the baron of the castle pictured on these pages has asked you to show a very important guest around the keep. Write a two- to three-minute speech, which explains the keep in detail, that you could use as you show around the baron's guest of honour.

3.4 Where have all our castles gone?

The great age of castle-building was between 1066 and about 1350. It was during this time that many of Britain's most famous castles were completed, including Warwick, Rochester, Kenilworth, Conwy, and, of course, the Tower of London.

But the vast majority of castles today are just empty ruins. Some of them have been so badly damaged that large parts of them are missing and many don't even have a roof! Some ruins are huge, and still look a bit like castles, but many others are just piles of old stones in a field. So what has happened to many of these once fine buildings? Why do many castles lie in a state of ruin? And what do we do to preserve and protect these places today?

Mission Objectives

- Discover how the use and look of castles has changed since the Middle Ages.
- Examine why the golden age of castle-building ended and what we do to protect castles today.

Changes to castles

Castles changed greatly over the years. Simple wooden towers on a mound of earth surrounded by fences and ditches were replaced by massive stone castles ringed by thick walls and deep moats. Later castles were more like palaces, designed for comfortable living rather than for protection and controlling land.

Castles in decline

There are two key reasons why the great age of castle-building stopped. First was the use of gunpowder in battle. Many of the castles were no match for the highly explosive impact of gunpowder on their walls.

Also, after 1500, Britain became more peaceful and there was less fighting… and the rich castle-owning nobles no longer needed to live in these big, cold, dark, draughty, damp buildings. Some lords made their castles into comfortable homes. They added extensions to them, often made out of brick and with large windows, and made pretty gardens around their castles. These changes continued over the years as the castle passed between different owners (see **Source A**). Other lords and barons moved out of their castles and built smaller, more comfortable homes nearby. They let the castles fall to ruin (see **Source B**).

SOURCE A: *A castle with modern extensions and renovations.*

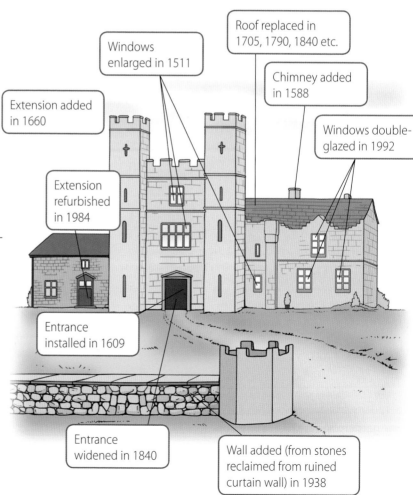

Windows enlarged in 1511

Roof replaced in 1705, 1790, 1840 etc.

Chimney added in 1588

Windows double-glazed in 1992

Extension added in 1660

Extension refurbished in 1984

Entrance installed in 1609

Entrance widened in 1840

Wall added (from stones reclaimed from ruined curtain wall) in 1938

Labels on the image:
- Visitors centre selling food and souvenirs
- Historical re-enactment showing what life was like in the Middle Ages
- Tourists
- Souvenirs bought from the visitors centre
- VISITORS CENTRE
- MAP OF CASTLE
- Guide books for sale
- Picnic area
- Map and history of the castle

Castles today

There are literally hundreds of castles dotted all over Britain. Whilst lots are now ruins, some have undergone dramatic restoration and have been converted into hotels and conference centres. Others are still privately owned and are used as homes.

Many, though, are looked after by groups and organizations such as English Heritage, Cadw and the National Trust. You can go and visit some of our finest castles, wander around the grounds, look through the display areas and gaze at medieval artefacts, models and old suits of armour. Sometimes there are demonstrations by knights on horseback or archers shooting arrows. Often they have a snack bar and a shop where you can buy a souvenir of your visit. Every year thousands of people visit Britain's castles – clearly there is still a huge interest in the way people lived in them.

Work

1 In your own words explain why, after 1350, castles were used less and less, and why many fell to ruin.

2 Think for yourself. How do organizations like English Heritage, Cadw and the National Trust look after Britain's castles today? You might like to discuss answers to this in a group before you write them down.

3 Look at **Source A**. Imagine you are an estate agent with the job of selling the castle. Create a set of notes to go with the picture to help sell the property.

You need to make sure you include why castles were built in Britain to begin with, what role they played in medieval history and how the castle has been changed, developed and extended over the years. You might want to add more pictures to your sales information.

Assessing Your Learning 1

What do we need to know about castles?

Good historians can bring together all the different things they've learned about a topic. This is your chance to have a go at doing this.

A website is being launched, designed to contain everything a young historian might need to know about medieval castles. The website will be made up of six sections covering each of the areas in the webpage below.

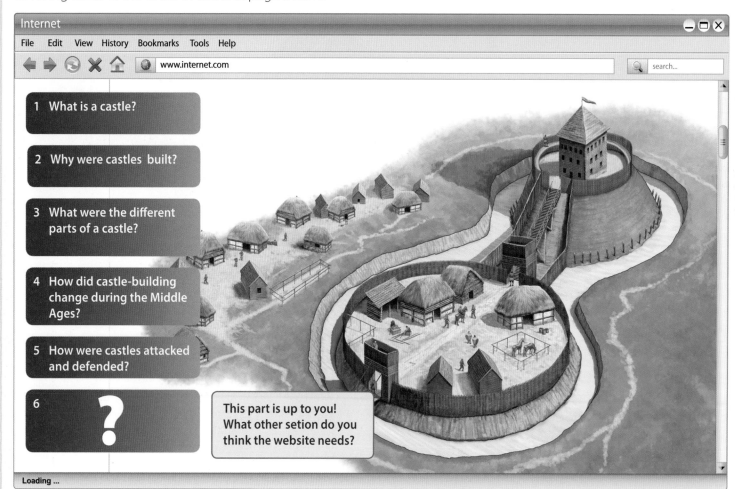

Internet

File   Edit   View   History   Bookmarks   Tools   Help

www.internet.com   search…

1   What is a castle?

2   Why were castles built?

3   What were the different parts of a castle?

4   How did castle-building change during the Middle Ages?

5   How were castles attacked and defended?

6   **?**

This part is up to you! What other setion do you think the website needs?

Loading …

As a History expert, you've been asked to write a summary of what you think should be included in each section. Your summaries should be no longer than 100 words each and will need to explain:

- The main facts and figures for that section. What are the important historical words and dates, for example?

- The key points you want to make. For example, in the 'How did castle-building change during the Middle Ages' section, you will need to say that wooden castles were replaced by stones ones… but you should also mention *why* this change took place.

Think about what pictures or diagrams you might use to help you with the points you make and the explanations you give. What pictures and diagrams might you use from this *Student Book*, for example?

What do I need to do now?

- Look back through the pages in this chapter that might help you.

- Select pages, dates, facts, figures, diagrams and explanations that might help you write your summaries, and then start drafting each summary.

- Remember, you need to think of a new section, of your own choice, to go onto the website (section 6). If the website is meant to contain everything a young historian needs to know about medieval castles, what else do you think is important enough to go on the website?

- You are writing six summaries in total, so keep them short, sharp and packed with information.

How to present your work

- You might show what each page will look like and how it might be set out. Perhaps use an A4 or A3 sheet of paper to show what each page will look like to someone viewing the site.

- You could present each summary as a mind-map – or how about presenting each summary in a PowerPoint presentation?

Assessing your work

In a **good** website, you would… **Good**	• describe what castles were, what they looked like and how they protected the people inside • explain how castles changed over the years (for example, from wood to stone) • include a list of diagrams and sources that could be used in each section • use dates and historical terms • choose a relevant topic for section six (your own choice).
In a **better** website, you would… **Better**	• describe what castles were, what they looked like and how they protected the people inside in **greater detail** • explain how castles changed and **give reasons why** these changes took place • include a **detailed** list of diagrams and sources that could be used in each section • use dates and historical terms correctly **at all times** • choose a relevant topic for section six and **give reasons** for your choice.
In the **best** website, you would… **Best**	• **accurately** describe what castles were, what they looked like and how they protected people using the correct historical terms and dates at all times • explain **in detail** how castles changed and how stone castles **developed** over the years (for example, the introduction of concentric castles) • **explain** why castle-building declined in the fifteenth century • **select, organize and use** relevant information and sources, as well as the correct historical dates and terms, at all times • choose a topic for section six and **justify** your choice by explaining why a student should know about it.

Hungry for More?

There is probably a medieval castle or some ruins in a town near you. Research and make a presentation on the castle, including:
- Who built it and when?
- Did any sieges take place there?

- Find out if it has any special features used to protect it from attack.
- Try to find out a little bit about who lived in the castle.
- Have you visited it? What was it like? How did you find out about its past?

Religious beliefs

Today, there are many different religions in Britain. Many people consider themselves Christian but only around three people in every hundred go to church on a Sunday. Things were very different in medieval Britain and religion was a much more important part of daily life. Over the next few pages, you will learn about the role of the Church in people's lives, how and why people worked for God, and why people became pilgrims.

Mission Objectives

- Investigate the importance of religion in medieval times.
- Evaluate the role of religion in everyday life.

Heaven and hell

In the Middle Ages almost everyone in Britain believed in God. They believed that heaven and hell were real places – as real as France or Spain – and where you ended up when you died depended on how you had lived your life.

God's will

People used religion to explain things. At a time when there was limited scientific knowledge about how the world worked, people looked to God for answers. Bad harvests, nasty illnesses and unfortunate accidents were viewed as punishments from God for sins that had been committed. But if you tried to lead a good life and went to church regularly, heaven was the reward that made up for the suffering on earth.

The heart of the village

The biggest building in a town or village would be the church. Churches were very noisy because they were used as meeting spaces. People didn't want to spend too much time in their tiny, smelly huts, with smoke from fires and the smell of animals! Children's games, plays and summer fairs were sometimes held in the churchyard. A church would have been a lively place, full of laughter, conversation and activity.

> 'In hell the wicked are tortured on burning trees. They were hung by the feet, or hands, or hair, or neck, or tongue, or arm. There is a horrible river, full of fish-like monsters which gobble up the souls of the wicked, who get what they deserve.'

▲ **SOURCE A:** *This is how a medieval priest described hell. People believed that if you committed crimes, didn't pray much and were a bad person, you would face these kinds of horrors.*

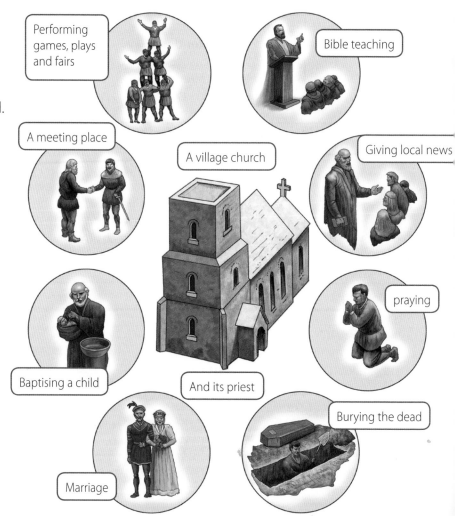

Performing games, plays and fairs

Bible teaching

A meeting place

A village church

Giving local news

praying

Baptising a child

And its priest

Burying the dead

Marriage

SOURCE B: *This diagram illustrates the functions of a village church and its priest.*

The priest

The village priest played a very important role in medieval society, and was part of most people's lives from the day they were born to the day they died. He was an advisor and a local leader. During confession the priest would listen while villagers told him of the sinful things they had done. At church services he would tell villagers that they would go to heaven if they were good but go to hell if they were bad. There were pictures, statues, stained glass, and paintings to remind people of this. Huge **doom paintings** showed angels welcoming good people into heaven and devils pulling murderers into pots of boiling oil in hell.

Pay up!

The villagers had to give the local church one tenth of all the food they grew. This was called the **tithe**. As you can imagine, the villagers were often unhappy about this, especially if the harvest was bad. Also, when someone died, the priest received their second-best working animal! For the peasants, worshipping God could be an expensive business.

Wise Up Words

doom painting   Pope   tithe

SOURCE C: *A doom painting from a medieval church in Chaldon, Surrey.*

Work

1 **a** Copy and complete the following paragraph. In the Middle Ages, almost everyone believed in _____ and went to _____. The local church was a busy place and children's games and summer _____ were sometimes held in the _____. People tried to lead good lives because they wanted to go to _____. They were afraid of _____ .

   b Villagers had to give the local church one tenth of their harvest as a tithe. What is this as a percentage?

2 Make a list of all a medieval priest's duties.

3 Study **Source C**.
   a Why was it important to have pictures and paintings on church walls in the Middle Ages? Clue: Think about the language used by the priest in his services.
   b What was the purpose of a doom painting? How do you think these kinds of paintings might affect the way someone behaved after leaving church?
   c Draw your own doom painting. Remember, it's got to tell people what will happen to them in heaven and hell, and must not include any words.

4.2 A day in the life of a monk

Some men decided to devote their whole lives to God. They left their families, homes and possessions and moved into a **monastery** as a **monk**. But what did they do when they got there? What rules did they live by to please God? How did they help the rest of society? And what made so many men become monks?

Mission Objectives

- Explain why some men became monks and what their daily life involved.
- Understand how monks contributed to medieval society.

Why take up the habit?

Monks first arrived in England in the sixth century, when Saint Augustine, a Benedictine monk, built the first monastery. In 1066, there were around 1000 monks in England – but this number quickly increased after William's invasion. By 1300, there were over 12,000 monks in England – meaning that out of every 150 people, one was a monk!

A monk's life was not an easy one. It was dominated by prayer – every three hours – day and night! They had to live by a strict set of rules set down by Saint Benedict (see below).

SOURCE A: The buildings where monks lived were called monasteries. A large monastery was called an abbey.

'Here everything is peaceful and quiet. We are free from all the noise and worry of the world. All the monks are very friendly and no one is selfish.'

▲ **SOURCE B:** This monk from Rievaulx Abbey wrote about the peace of a monk's life around 1170.

A good monk must:

Spend his life in service to God

Give away all of his property

Obey the abbot (head of the monastery) at all times

Wear a habit (robe), sandals and shave the top of his head (known as a tonsure)

Stay in the monastery until he dies.

Signed

Saint Benedict

Hungry for More?

Followers of Saint Benedict were called Benedictines. However, not all monks followed Saint Benedict's rules. See what you can find out about different types of monks.

Joining up

A boy could join a monastery as young as seven years of age. He would have been known as a novice. Why not read about a day in Novice Arthur's life below?

The diary of Novice Arthur, aged 13 ¾

What a busy day! Brother Gerald woke me up at two in the morning for an hour of prayers. It was so cold.

I was up again at six for more prayers. We then ate our breakfast of bread and ale in the refectory. Sometimes we have porridge, but not today! None of us are allowed to talk when we're eating... and you are beaten or whipped if you do.

At eight o'clock we met in the chapter house to sort out our work for the day. There's no choice, we are just told what to do. After a short, relaxing walk in the cloisters I went off to work in the *scriptorium*. I cut and smooth animal skins to make *vellum* to write on. Sometimes I copy out books and decorate the capital letters at the start of paragraphs. We prayed again at eleven o'clock and at midday ate our lunch of soup, bread and ale.

After more prayers I went out to tend the fruit and vegetables in the fields. We help the local people by occasionally providing them with food or even free medical care. Some of the monks know how to make medicines from herbs. When we don't feel well we go to the infirmary and are looked after by these clever monks. We also teach a few of the local children to read in our small school and collect clothing and money for the very poor.

We prayed again at six before supper... and then again afterwards. I've just polished my tonsure with a piece of stone to keep it free of hair. You get whipped if you don't. Sometimes you are given less food if you do not follow the rules! It's nine o'clock now and I'm off to bed in my dormitory. I have to be awake again at two o'clock...

Wise Up Words

chronicle   illuminated   manuscript   monastery
monk   scriptorium   vellum

SOURCE C: *This example of an illuminated manuscript comes from the Lindisfarne Gospels.*

Illuminating work

Monks were probably the best-educated people in medieval society and monasteries were important centres of learning. They acted as libraries for ancient books and **manuscripts**. Monks not only read these books, they also made sure the knowledge wasn't lost by copying them by hand. This took place in a special room called a scriptorium, a long narrow hall with booths placed against windows to help the monks see what they were doing. Valuable books were chained to the desk to prevent them being damaged if they were knocked off. Sometimes monks wrote their own books called **chronicles**. They also often **illuminated** their books with tiny, beautiful paintings around the edges of the page and on capital letters.

Work

1   Being a monk seems like a hard life to people today. Try to explain why you think so many men chose to lead this kind of life in the Middle Ages.

2   Read Novice Arthur's diary. Answer these questions.
   a   At what time did Arthur:
   •   get up for prayer?
   •   go to sleep at night?
   b   In what ways did monks in monasteries try to help local people? Why do you think they did this?
   c   Describe what went on in the refectory, scriptorium and infirmary.
   d   Name two types of punishment Arthur may have received in the monastery.

3   Using **Source C** as a guide, make your own illuminated manuscript. In it, explain why monks copied books and why this was important.

Was it fun to be a nun?

It wasn't just men who wanted to devote their lives to God, women did too. They became nuns, lived in nunneries and lived lives that were fairly similar to monks'. Nunneries were often built next to monasteries – and in the Middle Ages there were around 130 of them. There were not as many nuns as monks, though, and they hardly ever worked with books or manuscripts. So what did they do instead? How and why did women become nuns? And how did they help the rest of society?

Mission Objectives

- Examine why some women became nuns and what their lives involved.
- Explain how they helped the rest of society.

Joining a nunnery

Usually, women had to pay to become a nun. Sometimes a family might pay a fee (called a **dowry**) to a nunnery so that one of their daughters could become a nun.

Women became nuns for lots of reasons – and at various ages. Look at the stories below to find out why these three women joined a nunnery.

FACT!

Not every young woman was thrilled at the prospect of a life devoted to God. In 1318, a nun called Joanna from Clementhorpe nunnery faked her own death and staged her own funeral in an attempt to avoid being a nun for the rest of her life.

My name is Sister Emily and I'm 16 years old. When I was born, my mother and I nearly died. My father prayed to God and promised Him that I would spend my life doing His work if I lived. I did, so when I was a very young girl, my father kept his promise and handed me over to the sisters with a dowry.

My name is Sister Ursula and I'm 22 years old. When it was time for me to marry, I told my father that I didn't want a husband – I wanted to become a nun. That way, my education would continue and I would have responsibilities and jobs that are far more interesting than being a wife and mother. My father gave a dowry to the nunnery and I donated my silver necklace that belonged to my grandfather.

My name is Sister Winifred and I am 55 years old. I became a nun when my husband died two years ago. I decided to dedicate the rest of my life to God and gave all of my money and belongings, including my house, to the nunnery. Now I have nothing to worry about other than pleasing God and doing His work.

The Brides of Christ

After living as a nun for five years, nuns were **consecrated**. This involved a ceremony that was very similar to a wedding. The nun would have a ring placed on her finger and wore a wedding crown as she took her vows. From then on, she would be seen as being married to God, and so couldn't marry a man.

The daily life of a nun was very similar to that of a monk – it was based around prayer and chores, but was not quite as strict as life for the monks in the monasteries. Nuns often had their own possessions, wore jewellery, or kept a pet. Dogs were most popular – but some nuns kept monkeys!

Looking after the sick

Nuns were well known for caring for the sick and nunneries had special places where the sick could sleep and be looked after. In fact, the word 'hospital' comes from the Latin word 'hospitalis', which means 'a place for guests'. Between 1205 and 1300 there were over a hundred of these 'hospitals', as they became known, and most were attached to nunneries.

Wise Up Words

consecrated   dowry

'Care for the sick stands before everything. You must help them as Christ would, whom you really help by helping them… Also, you must be patient with them and you will gain greater merit with God. The sick should not be neglected at any single point.'

SOURCE A: *A picture of nuns looking after the sick in their nunnery. Nuns or sisters often attended to the sick – that's why senior nurses in hospitals today are known as 'sisters'.*

▲ **SOURCE B:** *Like some monks, nuns followed the rules of St Benedict. Some of these rules included how to look after the sick.*

Work

1. Identify the different reasons why each of the three sisters on the left-hand page became nuns.

2. Why do you think nuns were sometimes called 'Brides of Christ'?

3. 🖵 Look at **Source A**. Describe what you think is going on in the painting. Think about:
   - what the older nuns are showing the younger nuns
   - what the nun on the right is doing to the sick man
   - how the sick are treated.

4. Look at **Source B**.
   a. What did St Benedict say about caring for the sick?
   b. What evidence is there on these pages that nuns in the Middle Ages followed St Benedict's instructions?

5. Nunneries still exist all over the world, but there are far fewer now than there once were. Why do you think so few women want to become nuns today?

What were the Wars of the Cross?

Most people in medieval Europe had one thing in common – their religion. They were Christians and their religious leader on earth was the Pope. For Christians, Jerusalem was the most important city in the world. Jesus had lived there, and was crucified and buried there. Naturally, Christians wanted to visit Jerusalem so they could say they had been to a place that was so important in the life of Jesus. These travellers were known as **pilgrims**. Some pilgrims visited other places near to Jerusalem, such as Bethlehem, that were linked to the life of Jesus. In fact, the whole area became known as the Holy Land (see **Source A**).

Mission Objectives

- Summarize why some people in medieval Europe wished to visit the Holy Land.
- Discover why Jerusalem was an important city for Christians, Muslims and Jews.
- Examine why the Pope ordered the Crusades.

Not just Christians

The Holy Land was, and still is, important for many religions. Jews believe that Jerusalem is promised to them by God, and that it is their spiritual homeland. Jerusalem is also a holy site for Muslims because their leader, the Prophet Muhammad, is said to have visited the city and ascended from there to heaven. By the early Middle Ages, though, Arab Muslims controlled Jerusalem and allowed Jews and Christians to visit and live in the Holy Land… but in 1079 that all changed.

All change

In 1076 a tribe from the east, called the Turks, took over Jerusalem and the Holy Land. These Turks were Muslims who believed that no one but Muslims should set foot in the Holy Land. Christians who returned home from the Holy Land told stories about how they had been treated badly by the Turks. Some pilgrims were even killed. The Turks were also invading other land ruled by Christians.

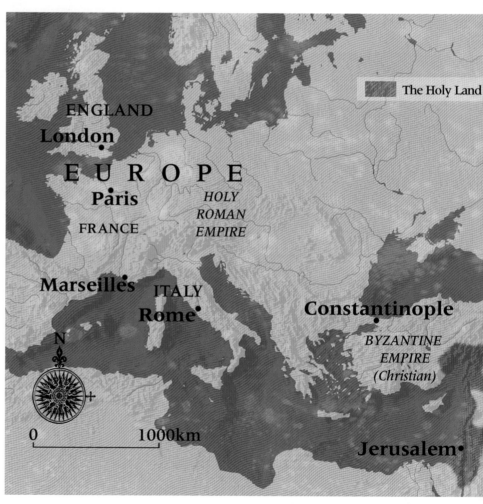

SOURCE A: *Europe and the Holy Land. As you can see, Christian pilgrims had to travel a long way to get to the Holy Land, where Jesus had lived.*

The Wailing or Western Wall is the last remaining part of King Herod's temple and is a site of pilgrimage for Jews.

The Dome of the Rock mosque is built on the site where Muslims believe the Prophet Muhammad rose up and visited heaven.

SOURCE B: *Jerusalem is a sacred city for three different faiths. It is because of this that people still struggle for control of Jerusalem to this day. In the Middle Ages it was very important to members of all three religions to secure safe access to their shrines.*

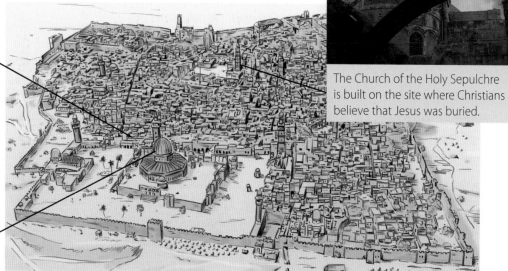

The Church of the Holy Sepulchre is built on the site where Christians believe that Jesus was buried.

A holy war

In 1095, the Christian leader, Pope Urban II, urged all Christian kings, lords, soldiers, and ordinary people to go and fight the Muslim Turks. He promised that anyone who died fighting would go straight to heaven. Thousands of people decided to go. They sewed crosses, the sign of Christianity, onto their clothes and flags. These journeys became known as the **Crusades**, which means 'wars of the cross'. Between 1096 and 1250 there were many Crusades against the Muslim Turks.

'*Brothers, I speak as a messenger from God… Your fellow Christians in the east desperately need help. The Saracens have attacked them and have pushed deep into Christian land. They are killing great numbers of Christians. They are destroying churches and land. In the name of God, I beg you all to drive out these foul creatures.*

Your own land has too many people. There is not much wealth here. The soil hardly grows enough to support you. Set out for Jerusalem. Take that land from the wicked infidel and make it your own.

If you die on the journey or if you are killed in a battle against these Saracens all your sins will be forgiven at once. God Himself has given me the power to tell you this.

Some of you have spent too much time fighting against your fellow Christians. But now you must fight the Saracens. Let bandits become soldiers. Soldiers who have been fighting for money must now fight for heavenly riches.'

▲ **SOURCE C:** *Part of the speech made by Pope Urban II in 1095. 'Saracen' is a word for Muslims in the Middle Ages. 'Infidel' was a word used to describe non-Christians.*

Work

1 Explain why Jerusalem is an important city for:
   a Muslims   b Christians   c Jews.

2 Look at **Source C**.
   a Who said this?
   b Why was this man important to Christians?
   c How does the writer of this source try to encourage people to go on the Crusades? Make a list.

3 Design a poster for the Pope that would encourage people to leave their homes and fight in the Crusades. It must tell people why the Pope wants them to fight and what benefits are in it for them. Think about what illustrations you will put on your poster. Which words and phrases said by Pope Urban II will you use?

Wise Up Words

Crusades   infidel   pilgrim   Saracen

Cuthbert the Crusader

Meet Cuthbert, the second oldest son of his father, who is a rich and powerful English landowner. Cuthbert is a knight who is about to leave England and travel to the Holy Land with his fellow Crusaders. On his journey through Europe he'll be joined by thousands of people including fellow knights, lords, peasants, kings, wives, and even children. But what are their **motives** for going? Firstly, look at the wide variety of reasons for going on a Crusade given below.

Mission Objectives

- Categorize reasons why people went on Crusades.
- Evaluate a number of different routes to the Holy Land.

It was a chance for a knight to become a hero. One French knight wrote to his wife and said, 'It breaks my heart to leave you but in the Holy Land I will win praise and your true love.'

The Holy Land was rich with luxuries such as gold, spices and perfumes. One knight wrote in 1098, 'My dear wife, I now have twice as much silver and gold as when I set off.'

Shield made from wood covered with leather

Many people went because they felt it was their duty to obey the Pope, who had urged people to go.

The Pope promised to forgive all a person's sins if they went on a Crusade.

Some felt it was their Christian duty to make sure that fellow Christian pilgrims could travel to the Holy Land in peace, without being attacked by Muslim Turks.

Tunic, usually white with a red cross sewn on it

Some kings promised to reward fellow Crusaders with lands and titles.

Some younger knights went to try and get land overseas. This was tempting for people who, like Cuthbert, were not an eldest son, and so wouldn't inherit land.

Some people went to see the world and saw it as a great adventure.

FACT!

During the time of the Crusades, there was religious hatred in some parts of Europe. In 1189 and 1190, angry mobs attacked and killed Jews living in London and York. And in 1290, all Jews were expelled from England by King Edward I.

Some kings encouraged violent and aggressive knights to go on Crusades to get them out of the country.

Chain mail suit covering the whole body

Sword, up to 1.2 metres long

Crusaders paid no taxes while they were away and any money they owed didn't have to be paid until they returned.

So how would Cuthbert and his Crusaders get there?

The journey to the Holy Land was long and difficult. Travelling across land took a long time, and there were bandits and robbers to contend with. Travelling by boat was quicker, but there was the danger of shipwreck or attack by pirates. **Source A** shows some possible choices for Cuthbert and his Crusaders – but which one should he choose?

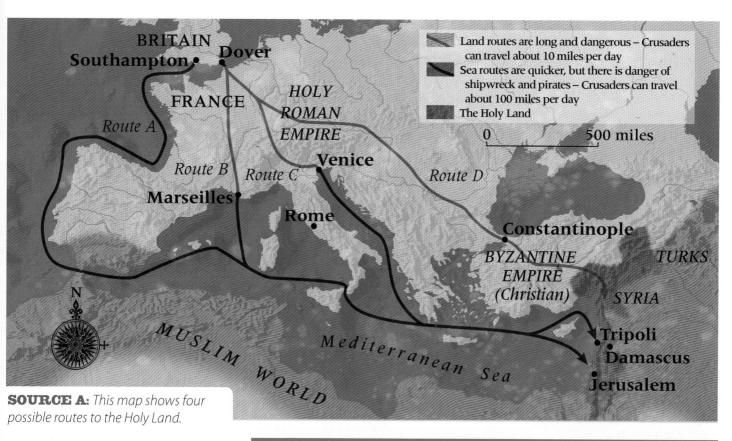

SOURCE A: *This map shows four possible routes to the Holy Land.*

Map legend:
- Land routes are long and dangerous – Crusaders can travel about 10 miles per day
- Sea routes are quicker, but there is danger of shipwreck and pirates – Crusaders can travel about 100 miles per day
- The Holy Land

0 — 500 miles

Labels on map: BRITAIN, Southampton, Dover, FRANCE, Route A, Route B, Route C, Marseilles, Rome, Venice, HOLY ROMAN EMPIRE, Route D, Constantinople, BYZANTINE EMPIRE (Christian), TURKS, SYRIA, Tripoli, Damascus, Jerusalem, MUSLIM WORLD, Mediterranean Sea, N

Be a Top Historian

Top historians know that there are nearly always lots of different reasons why people do things. And different people will have different reasons for taking part in the same event – like the Crusades. Sometimes, though, you can put the reasons into categories, such as religious reasons or financial reasons, for example.

Work

1 Look at **Source A**.

  a Imagine you are Cuthbert. You have four possible routes to the Holy Land (Route A, B, C, or D). What are the advantages and disadvantages of each route?

  b Work out how long each journey will take using the scale on the map (this will be an approximate time).

  c Which route would take the longest?

  d Which route would take the least time?

  e So which route should you choose? Give reasons for your choice.

2 a Look at the ten different reasons why people decided to go on a Crusade. Try to sum up each of the ten reasons in only THREE words.

  b Try to place each of the ten reasons (which should now be summarized in three words or fewer) in one of the following categories:

  | Religion | Money | Power | Other |

  c Why do you think it's important to know that people had different motives for going on Crusades?

Chronicles of the Crusades

The age of the Crusades lasted for 300 years. Time and time again, Christian armies set off from Europe to fight for control of Jerusalem and the Holy Land. There were victories and defeats on both sides. But what were the key battles, who were the key individuals, and who had gained control of the Holy Land by the time the Crusades ended?

Mission Objectives

- Define the period in history known as 'The Crusades'.
- Construct a timeline of key events.
- Interpret views on Saladin.

1. First Crusade, 1096–1099

An army of peasants, led by a man called Peter the Hermit, was the first group to set off for the Holy Land. They were nearly all killed. An army of knights followed led by Robert of Normandy, the eldest son of William the Conqueror. After many fierce, bloody, brutal battles they captured Jerusalem in 1099. It remained in Christian hands for the next 88 years!

2. Second Crusade, 1145–1149

The knights of the First Crusade then swept through the Holy Land creating Christian kingdoms and building castles. But in 1144, the Muslims began to take back land. King Louis VII of France set off to regain the land… but was defeated at Damascus.

'Saladin spent much of his time drinking and gambling. When he became leader of the Muslims he took over places by force or trickery. This greedy tyrant then took the Holy Land.'

▲ **SOURCE B:** *Written by an English monk in the thirteenth century.*

SOURCE C: *From a description of Saladin, written by a Muslim who knew him.* ▼

'Saladin was so determined to fight the Holy War he thought of nothing else. Saladin made sure that his men were fed and cared for. He never said bad things about people.'

SOURCE A: *This picture shows Crusaders attacking Jerusalem in 1099.*

3. Third Crusade, 1189–1192

In 1174, the Muslims began to unite under one leader – Salah ad-Din (known to the Crusaders as 'Saladin'). In 1187, his army recaptured Jerusalem and took other land controlled by Christians. The Crusaders (who included King Richard I of England) captured the town of Acre, but quarrelled amongst themselves and failed to capture Jerusalem. On 2 September 1192, King Richard met with Saladin and made a deal – Jerusalem could remain in Muslim hands, but Christians could visit without coming to any harm (see **Sources B** and **C**).

4. Fourth Crusade, 1202–1204

The Pope (Innocent III) asked all Christians to capture Jerusalem once again. But the Crusaders never reached the Holy Land because different groups fell out with each other on the way. In the end, Christians fought other Christians!

6. Fifth, Sixth and Seventh Crusades, 1217–1250

All of these Crusades failed to re-take Jerusalem and were unable to repeat the success of the First Crusade.

7. Crusade of Nicopolis, 1396

At the Battle of Nicopolis (in modern-day Bulgaria), an army of French, Hungarian and German knights were defeated. This is sometimes called 'the Last Crusade'.

5. Children's Crusade, 1212

Some historical accounts say this Crusade was led by a 12-year-old French shepherd boy named Stephen. Up to 30,000 children are said to have left for the Holy Land determined to succeed where the adults had failed. Tragically, many died from hunger and exhaustion on the way. Others returned home, but thousands were kidnapped and sold as slaves. However, no one knows what really happened, or which parts of the story are true.

FACT!

The European Crusaders called the Muslim Turks 'Saracens', which is from the Greek word for Muslim. Muslims used the word 'Franks' to describe the Crusaders as they believed most of them came from France.

Work

1 a Put the following dates in chronological order and explain what happened in each year.

   1202; 1099; 1096; 1145; 1192; 1396; 1144; 1212; 1174; 1189; 1187

   b Think about what is meant by the term 'turning point'. Do you think any of the events that happened on these dates could be called 'turning points'? Explain your choices.

2 Look at **Source A**.
   a What are the attackers doing? (Look at what they are doing to the people of Jerusalem too!)
   b What impression does this give of Crusaders and their reasons for going on a Crusade?
   c This source wasn't painted until the 1300s, but it shows an attack in 1099. Does this mean it may not be useful to a historian?

3 Look at **Sources B** and **C**.
   a Write a sentence describing what the writer of **Source B** thought about Saladin.
   b Write a sentence describing what the writer of **Source C** thought about Saladin.
   c Can you explain why the two opinions are so different?
   d Why do different opinions sometimes make the study of history so challenging?

4 In no more than 150 words, explain which side you think won the Crusades. You must include examples of both Crusader and Muslim victories and explain who controlled the Holy Land when the Crusades came to an end.

What did the Crusades do for us?

There were lots of battles and wars during the time of the Crusades. But there were also times when there was peace and Christians and Muslims mixed with each other. As a result, all sorts of ideas from the two different cultures were exchanged. So what were these ideas? How did they affect life in Europe? And which side seemed to learn the most?

Mission Objectives

- Understand how life in Europe changed and improved after contact with the Muslim world.
- Decide which change was most important and why.

Before the Crusades

New products

Crusaders brought back lots of things from the Holy Land. These included foods such as lemons, melons, apricots, sugar, syrup and spices like nutmeg and cinnamon. Cotton, silk and slippers changed the way people dressed. Muslims used pigeons to carry messages too – something that was copied in Europe.

The Muslims had been in contact with Christians from Europe long before the Crusades began. Muslims had conquered Spain in the seventh century and had traded with some of their European neighbours for centuries. But Christians from northern European countries like Germany, France and England had not had contact with the Muslims. They had very little respect for the Muslims at first and thought they were a godless, uncivilized people. They were in for a surprise! In times of peace, in between the fighting, the two sides mixed. Without a doubt the Christians learned the most!

Technology

The Muslims thought that studying and education were very important. Because of this, they had made advances in science and technology that amazed the Christians. These included mirrors, the magnetic compass, the magnifying glass, and a tool that could measure the distance between stars. The Muslims had also made advances in sailing and improved surgical tools.

Knowledge

The Muslims used a number system that made complicated mathematics far easier. In fact, Arabic numbers are the ones we use today. The Muslims also had better maps. The works of the Ancient Greeks, which had been lost in Europe, had been translated by the Muslims. This meant that the ideas of Plato and Socrates could be re-discovered by the Europeans.

Warfare

The Muslims used archers a lot. European armies, especially the English, started to use archers a lot too. They also copied Muslim castle designs and a weapon used to attack castles called a trebuchet, which was like a huge catapult.

SOURCE A: *The Crusaders learned the game of shah (or shatranj), which they called chess, from the Muslims.*

Work

1 Look at the diagram on the left-hand page.
  a List all the things that they learned from fighting the Muslims.
  b Now list all the things that they learned from living peacefully and talking to the Muslims.
  c Which list is longer – fighting or talking? Explain why you think this is.
  d Of all the things that Christians learned from the Crusades, which do you think was most important? Give reasons for your answer.

2 Look at **Sources B**, **C**, **D**, and **E**.
  a For each source, explain in your own words the point that the writer is trying to make.
  b What impression do these sources give you of relationships between some Muslims and Christians?
  c If you were trying to find out about the Crusades, why would it be a bad idea to read only stories written by either a Muslim or a Christian? Why?

3 Look at the diagram that shows how much the Christians learned from the Muslims (page 70). Design a poster to show what the Crusaders learned and brought back from the Holy Land. You cannot use more than 15 words on your poster, but someone looking at it should be able to understand the importance of the Crusades.

'When I used to enter the Aqsa Mosque, which was occupied by the Christian Crusaders who were my friends, they would leave so that I might pray in it. One day I entered this Mosque, said Allah is great and stood up in the act of praying. Upon this one of the Franks rushed on me, got hold of me and turned my face eastward. "This is the way thou should pray!" he said. A group of Christians seized him and repelled him from me. They apologised to me saying: "This is a stranger who has only recently arrived from the land of the Franks. He has never before seen anyone praying except eastward".'

▲ **SOURCE B:** *From a book written in the twelfth century by Usamah ibn Munqidh , a rich Muslim from Damascus.*

'We who were Westerners find ourselves transformed into inhabitants of the East. The Italian or Frenchman of yesterday has become a citizen of the Holy Land. We have already forgotten our native land. Some men have already taken Syrian women as wives. Races utterly unlike each other live together in trust.'

▲ **SOURCE C:** *Written by a Frenchman, Fulcher of Chartres, in around 1120.*

'A man was accused of a crime, so they dropped him in water. Their idea was that if he was innocent he would sink, but if he was guilty he would float. This man did his best to sink but he could not do it. He was found guilty and they pierced his eyes with red hot metal – may Allah's curse be upon them.'

▲ **SOURCE D:** *Usamah ibn Munqidh writing about the way some Christians held trials to find out if someone was guilty or not.*

'These people study no science and are more like animals than human beings. Those who live in England are so far away from the sun that they have become stupid.'

▲ **SOURCE E:** *A Muslim scholar's opinion of the English Christian invaders.*

What was life like in a medieval village?

Most people live in towns and cities today. In the Middle Ages, things were different. Although towns existed, there weren't many of them, and the vast majority of people lived and worked in villages. So what were these villages like?

Mission Objectives

- Investigate village life during the Middle Ages.
- Describe how a medieval villager spent his day.

Life in a medieval village was tough. The peasant villagers (known as **villeins**) worked out in the fields from sunrise to sunset whenever there was work to do. Most of the land was owned by someone else (the lord of the manor) who was usually a knight or baron. The lord let the peasants live on his land in return for their obedience, a payment, and several days of work from them per week.

The peasant families lived in wooden huts that they would build themselves. Each had a small garden where they grew vegetables and fruit. They might also keep sheep, pigs, goats, and chickens.

The fields that surrounded the village were carefully divided up into strips and shared out amongst the villagers, so that no one peasant had all the good land or all the bad land. Out in the fields they grew wheat for bread, barley for beer, and oats and rye to feed the animals. There were no shops or supermarkets as we know them today, so most of the food they needed had to be grown by the peasants themselves. If there was a bad harvest or their animals died, the villagers could starve to death.

However, not everyone in the village farmed. Some had a specialist job such as blacksmith, carpenter, or cloth weaver. They would sell their goods and services to other people – or even travel to the nearest town or neighbouring village to sell things on market days.

Common land: Cattle were allowed to graze here

Church

Blacksmith's workshop: he made pots, pans, chains, and knives

Carpenter's workshop: he made carts, axe handles, and wheels

Village green: used as a meeting place and for markets

Village pub ale and a sing popular way

Mill: people ground their corn into flour at the watermill. Peasants had to pay the lord to use it

River: villeins had to pay the lord to fish in the river

Work

1 ✏️ **Interview with…**

If you could travel back in time and meet with someone who lived in the village pictured on these pages, what interview questions would you ask them? How would you describe where **you** live to them? What are the main differences? Are there any similarities?

Castle: this dominated the area

Woodland: peasants gathered firewood here, but only the lord could hunt in it

Open fields divided equally into strips: each peasant had one or two strips in each field

The tithe barn: peasants had to give 10 per cent of what they grew to the priest; this was called a **tithe** and the produce was kept here

Manor house: the landowner lived here with his family; all the peasants made payments to him and worked on his land

Beehives: honey was one of the only methods of sweetening things

Peasant houses

Peasant's vegetable patch

What was life like in a medieval village?

What were the villagers' homes like?

The villages varied in size. Some contained fewer than ten houses, but larger ones might have over 50 homes as well as the lord's manor house, a church, a mill, and workshops for a blacksmith or a carpenter. Look at the diagram and sources on these pages to discover what a typical peasant cottage was like and how a peasant villager lived his life.

Where do they live? In a one-room hut. The frame is made from wood and the walls are made from **wattle** (sticks woven together) and **daub** (mud, dung and straw – see **Source B**). The windows are holes in the wall covered by shutters and the floor is made of mud mixed with straw and ox blood to make it hard. There is a hole in the roof to let out the smoke from the fire inside. The animals live in the hut too… what a smell! Water for cooking and cleaning comes from a well or river and outside is a hole dug in the ground that is used as a toilet.

How does this villager spend his day? He gets up when it's light enough to see and works all day. In the spring he ploughs the land and plants seeds. In the summer he harvests the hay, weeds the corn, and scares the birds. In the autumn he harvests the corn and kills and salts some animals for winter. In the winter he clears away any wasteland, repairs his hut and tools and, most importantly, tries to keep warm.

Could the villeins leave the village? No, they weren't allowed to because the lord owned them. And if they did run off they could be tried in court and punished. However, villeins were sometimes given their freedom by a kind or grateful lord – or they could buy their freedom if they saved up enough money.

What do they eat?
- Breakfast – 6am. Bread and ale to drink (water wasn't safe).
- Lunch – 10am. Bread, perhaps an egg, a piece of fish, or cheese. Ale to drink.
- Supper – 4pm. Bread and pottage (a thick vegetable soup). Ale to drink.

What about his wife? She works as hard as he does. She cooks, cleans, and looks after the children. She fetches water, makes and mends clothes, and helps out in the fields when she is needed.

SOURCE A: *This image of a medieval farmer tending to his field is an illustration from a medieval manuscript.*

SOURCE B: *The walls of the hut were made from wattle and daub. The wattle is the framework of sticks and twigs woven together. The daub is the plaster (made from mud, animal dung and straw) that is smeared on top of this to make a wall.*

'The poorest folk are our neighbours… in their hovels, overburdened with children… whatever they save by spinning they spend on rent, or on milk and oatmeal for food. And they themselves are often famished with hunger and wretched with the miseries of winter – cold, sleepless nights, when they get up to rock the cradle cramped in a corner, and rise before dawn to card and comb the wool, to wash and scrub and mend, and wind yarn and peel rushes for their rushlights… while the Friars feast on roast venison, they have bread and thin ale, with perhaps a scrap of cold meat or stale fish… I tell you, it would be a real charity to… comfort these cottagers along with the blind and the lame.'

▲ **SOURCE C:** *The view of a medieval writer who wanted rich people to treat the villeins a bit better. From* The Vision of Piers Plowman *by William Langland, written around 1390.*

Work

1 Draw a table like the one below, putting the following headings down the left-hand side:

windows; number of rooms; cooking; floor; heating; water supply; toilets; washing; walls

	A villein's home	My home
Windows	Holes in wall, shutters	Glass, curtains
Number of rooms	One	
Cooking		

Then fill in the table to show the key differences between your home and a medieval peasant's house.

2 Look at **Source C**.
   a Sum up what the writer is saying about a villein's life.
   b Why might the writer have been so keen to make a villein's life sound so terrible?
   c Do you think we can trust what the writer has written? Explain your answer carefully.

3 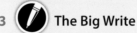 **The Big Write**

Imagine you are a villein in a medieval village. Write a description of a day in your life. Here are some ideas to think about:
   - How do you typically spend your day?
   - What is your house like?
   - Does your working day change throughout the year?
   - Where will you work or visit?
   - What sort of people will you meet?
   - Is there a particular type of food you enjoy?
   - At what times do you eat?

What was life like in a medieval town?

People who didn't live in villages in the countryside, or in castles, lived in towns. When William conquered England in 1066 there were only about 15 towns with a population of more than 1000 people, and only about eight with more than 3000 living there. London was the largest with about 10,000 people, followed by Winchester and Norwich with about 3000 people each. Most people (about 90 per cent of the population) lived in small villages out in the countryside, with no more than 50 to 100 people in each.

Mission Objectives

- Explain what life was like in a medieval town and what a town might look like.
- Discover why towns grew.
- Assess how buying and selling was organized.

Why towns developed

After 1066, towns began to grow. Some villages grew in size too – and became towns! Sometimes towns grew where major roads met or near a bridge where people came to buy and sell goods. Others grew near a castle or monastery. The local lord still owned these places, but, if the town continued to grow and the townspeople made lots of money, they might join together and buy their land and freedom from the lord or king.

Town charters

A town's freedom, written down on a special piece of paper known as a charter, gave the townspeople the chance to run the town themselves. In fact, by 1400, about 300 towns had received their charter and freedom. By this time, London's population had grown to over 40,000.

The diagram on these pages shows a typical town in about 1250. Look for the following:

1 Most streets were just dirt tracks

2 A pedlar selling goods as he walks through the streets

3 The castle – at one time only the castle was here, but over the years the town was built in front of it

4 Shops had picture signs to show what they sold because few people could read

5 Large private house, probably the home of a **merchant**

6 Defensive tower and guardpoint

7 Entrance gate – guarded by sentries 24 hours a day, seven days a week

8 Having fun – all sorts of people might entertain the townspeople in return for a few coins

9 A young apprentice being taught the skills of a trade by a master craftsman; the training lasted seven years

10 The market – held once or twice a week, people came from the countryside to sell eggs, cheese, butter, fruit, and vegetables

11 Many houses had vegetable gardens

12 Market stalls – merchants brought exotic goods, such as spices and silks, from abroad

13 Meeting rooms above the gateway

14 Traders bringing in goods by river

15 A wagon bringing goods to sell at the market

16 The Guildhall – where the town **guild** met. This was a group of traders and craftsmen that made rules for its members to follow; they set prices, organized training and made sure goods were well made

17 Town walls patrolled by guards

Wise Up Words

charter   export   guild   merchant

> *Town Charter*
> *The king gives the officials running this town permission to:*
>
> 1. *RENT LAND for their own use without working for the lord*
>
> 2. *HOLD MARKETS every week without paying taxes to the lord*
>
> 3. *HOLD FAYRES every year*
>
> 4. *FIX PRICES for goods sold at market*
>
> 5. *HOLD COURTS to punish traders who break the rules of the market*
>
> 6. *HAVE THE RIGHT OF GALLOWS – to punish criminals by hanging.*

▲ **SOURCE A:** *A typical* **charter** *granted by a king or local lord in the Middle Ages. Both Leeds and Liverpool became towns in 1207 after receiving their charter.*

Work

1 List the main reasons why some towns grew.

2 Look at **Source A**.
   a What is a charter?
   b What advantages were there in having a charter for:
      i the townspeople?
      ii the local Lord or King?

Look through all the sources on these pages to discover what life was like in a medieval town.

SOURCE A: *Market stalls around a town wall, as shown in a manuscript from 1458. Can you see what customers are buying?*

wood	*leather*
fish	*silk*
grain	*wine*
hawks	*soap*
lead	*farm animals*
furs	*canvas*
spices	*glass*
rope	*wool*
salt	

▲ **SOURCE B:** *Goods for sale at Boston Fair in 1250. Some goods like wool, leather and fish would have been produced locally. Other goods like furs, rope and wine would have been imported from abroad.*

'Traders can be found in their particular areas each morning. There is wine for sale on the river bank. Every day you may find food, dishes of meat – roast, fried and boiled; fish; cheap cuts of meat for the poor and more expensive for the rich... Just outside the town there is a field called Smith-field. On every sixth day of the week there is a sale of fine horses... In another part of the field are things brought to market by the country folk – farming tools, pigs, milk, cows, large oxen and woolly sheep, mares to pull the plough and young foals.'

◀ **SOURCE C:** *William Fitzstephen's 'Description of the city of London', from around 1174; Britain's most important* **export** *at this time was wool. It was sold by farmers and traders abroad where it was made into cloth. Some was made into cloth in Britain too. Fortunes were made from the wool trade and it has been estimated that by 1300 there were up to 18 million sheep in Britain (and around 3-4 million people).*

Henry the lead beater
Robert the cook
Hugh the carpenter
Thomas the painter
Hugh the hosier
William the builder
William the butter maker
William the cutler
John the cordwainer
John the thatcher
Pagen the miller
Richard the combere
Robert the baker
William the belt maker
William the skinner
Richard the saddler
Edward the weaver

▲ **SOURCE D:** *Craftsmen in Coventry in 1250.*

Combere – prepared wool for clothmaking
Cordwainer – made boots
Cutler – made knives
Hosier – made stockings
Skinner – took skins off animals
Thatcher – made house roofs from straw or reeds
Weaver – made cloth

▲ **SOURCE E:** *Medieval trades and their names.*

Poor workmanship will be punished by a fine and goods will be confiscated.
Shoemakers Guild, Chester

No one shall make or sell hats within the city unless he has special permission.
Hatmakers Guild, London

If the threads of the cloth are too far apart, the cloth and the tools used will be burned.
Weavers Guild, Bristol

If by chance a member of the guild shall become poor through old age, accident or sickness, then he shall have seven pence (3p) from the guild every week.
Tanners Guild (leather workers), London

▲ **SOURCE F:** *Guild rules from a variety of towns.*

Work

1 Look at the picture of a town on the previous page and at **Source A** opposite. Imagine you live ten miles away from town. For the first time ever, your parents are taking you into town, and it is the most exciting day of your life – there are lots of new (and strange) sights, sounds and smells. Describe your visit.

2 Look at **Source C**.
   a Where in London would you be able to buy:
      i wine?
      ii sheep?
   b In larger towns (like London, Bristol and York), different parts of the town were used by traders selling the same thing. For example, all the silversmiths might be in Silver Street. What traders might you have expected to find in the following streets:
      • Baker Street, Cutler Row, Pudding Lane, Gold Street, Brewhouse Lane, Vine Street and Tanners Lane?
   c What advantages might there be in having all the traders close together, for:
      i the buyer?
      ii the sellers?

3 Look at **Sources D** and **E**.
   Copy and complete the following chart placing the name of the correct tradesman in each column.

Building	Making things to eat	Making things to wear	Other

4 Look at **Source F** and label 16 on page 77.
   a What was a guild?
   b Why do you think some of the guild rules were so strict?
   c Why do you think the guild chose to give money to their members who became poor because of old age, sickness or accident?

Hungry for More?

Many of our surnames today come from jobs and trades that people did long ago – names such as Cooper, Miller, Shearer and Carpenter, for example.
Try to find ten more surnames that come from medieval trades.

How smelly were the Middle Ages?

We know today that dirt and rubbish are home to germs and disease. From an early age we are taught to avoid germs by washing our hands regularly, clearing up rubbish, flushing toilets, brushing our teeth, and keeping ourselves clean. Our houses are full of cleaning products too; all are designed to make our clothes cleaner and our work surfaces germ-free! However, medieval people knew nothing of germs – not because they were stupid, they just didn't have the microscopes through which they could have seen them. As a result, people in the Middle Ages were a lot less fussy about living in smelly and dirty places than we are today. So just how smelly were the Middle Ages?

Mission Objectives

- Explore how and why standards of cleanliness and personal hygiene were very different from today.

How clean is your castle?

Even rich people in their castles still lived a pretty smelly life. Only the very rich had a bath regularly, usually in a big wooden tub lined with cloth. There *was* soap, but it wasn't very effective because it was usually made from animal fat and wood ash. King John, for example, bathed once a month and was charged five pence by the man who organized it. This doesn't sound a lot but it was the same amount that a labourer earned in a week!

What about toilets?

A castle's toilets were little more than holes with stone or wooden seats. The lord usually had his own at the top of the castle, next to where he slept, and torn strips of cloth were used instead of toilet paper. Often the toilets (or **garderobes** as they were known) were built on different floors, one above the other. The sewage dropped down chutes straight into the moat (see **Source A**). If there was no moat, the sewage emptied into a pit, which had to be cleaned out by hand by the castle's gong farmer (see page 50)!

Poor peasants

Ordinary peasants struggled to keep clean too. Their cottages had no floorboards or carpets, just earth covered with straw. Windows – if they had any – were holes in the wall with a wooden shutter to keep out the wind. In the centre of the room was a fire, its smoke escaping through a hole in the roof. A medieval peasant must have always smelled of smoke – or even worse during the winter when they brought their animals inside and out of the cold! There were no taps to provide clean water for washing or drinking either; it had to be fetched from a stream, a river or a well. And there were no toilets, just a bucket in the corner of the room or a hole dug outside.

SOURCE A: *A diagram of how a castle toilet system might have worked.*

A load of rubbish

In the towns, life was just as smelly. There was no organized collection of rubbish in medieval times. Instead, people just tipped their rubbish into the streets or dumped it into a pit and let it rot away. There were no drains or sewage pipes to carry away dirty water either. At night, people went to the loo in pots. The next day they tipped the waste out of the window into the street below! In London, there was a public toilet. It was located on London Bridge and emptied straight into the River Thames below!

> 'The butchers were often the worst. They used to throw out any waste and let the animals' blood run along the road. In hot weather, the smell was terrible. Townspeople still kept animals, which could be fed on the land around the town. But often they let their pigs roam around the streets, looking for food in the gutters. There were chickens too. And rats.'

▲ **SOURCE B:** *A modern historian writing about the sorry state of the streets.*

> 'Next case: the lane called Ebbegate. This was a right of way [a public footpath] until it was blocked by Thomas Wytte and William de Hockele. They built toilets which stuck out from the walls of their houses. From these toilets human dung falls onto the heads of passers-by.'

▲ **SOURCE C:** *Notes from a court case in 1321. Thomas Wytte, an owner of a house, and William de Hockele were taken to court because of their toilets. In another court case from 1347, two men were found guilty of piping their own sewage into their next door neighbour's cellar.*

Getting better?

Although houses didn't have bathrooms or running water, it would be wrong to think that all people were permanently filthy. Some towns had public 'bath houses' where you could have a wash for a small fee, and a few places even employed **scavengers** to remove the filth. Some people also began to make the connection between rubbish and disease too. Although they didn't know about germs (they thought it was the bad smells from the rubbish that carried infection), it still led to England's first national health law in 1388 (see **Source D**).

> 'So much dung and filth and rubbish is thrown in ditches, rivers and other waters that the air is greatly infected and many illnesses and terrible diseases do daily happen. It is decreed, as well in London as in other cities and towns throughout England, that all they who throw dung, garbage, guts and other rubbish in ditches, rivers and other places shall have to remove, empty, or carry away, or pay to our Lord the King a fine of £20.'

▲ **SOURCE D:** *The English Sanitary Act, 1389.*

Wise Up Words

garderobe   scavenger

What Happened When?

All this rubbish attracted rats, which spread the killer disease, Black Death. Black Death ravaged towns and villages from 1348.

Work

1. **a** Think about your own personal hygiene. What have you done over the last few days to keep yourself clean, tidy and as germ-free as possible? Make a list.
   b Look at your list. Underline the things that people in medieval times would not have been able to do.
   c Give reasons why people in the Middle Ages were not as clean as we are today.

2. Who was cleaner – the rich or the poor? Give reasons for your answer.

3. 📄 Imagine you have been asked to create a leaflet to inform a group of foreign visitors coming to medieval England. What can they expect to find 'when nature calls'? Explain about toilets in castles, towns and villages. You might like to consider:
   - what toilet facilities they would expect to find in a castle
   - how castle toilets differed from those in the towns and villages.

Could you have fun in the Middle Ages?

In the Middle Ages, ordinary people didn't really have holidays. Instead, there were a number of feast days through the year, such as Easter Day, May Day, Midsummer's Eve, Christmas, and various Saints' days. On these days, after going to a church service, they would have some free time for themselves. In fact, our word 'holiday' comes from the term 'holy day'. And people generally made their own fun, creating home-made equipment with whatever they had to hand. Some of the sports and games were so popular that they are still enjoyed today.

Mission Objectives

- Investigate how both rich and poor spent their spare time in the Middle Ages.
- Categorize some of the major differences between sport today and sport in the Middle Ages.

So how did ordinary people enjoy their holy days?

Conkers
An early form of conkers became popular after 1066. The rules were simple – find a cobnut, drill a hole in it and thread it onto a piece of string. Then, taking turns, try and smash your opponent's cobnut to bits.

Mob football
No rules, no referee and as many players as you can get. Whole villages would play each other, with the goals several miles apart.

Ice skating
People would strap sharpened bones to their feet to use as skates. Archaeologists have found the skeleton of a young boy with his skates still strapped on his feet. Thin ice perhaps?

Bowling
Players would take it in turns to knock down as many skittles as they could with three balls.

Golf
Using a few basic clubs, players would hit a leather ball stuffed with hair. Popular in Scotland and Holland by 1500.

Shin hacking
Two villagers would kick each other in the shins as hard as they could until one of them couldn't take the pain and gave up.

Cold hand
A player would be blindfolded in front of a crowd and slapped by one of them. He or she would have to guess who hit them – and if they guessed correctly, it would be the 'slapper's' turn to be blindfolded. This was sometimes called 'blind man's buff' or 'hot cockles'.

Cock fighting
Two birds were forced to attack each other, sometimes with metal tied to their claws. People would bet on the result.

What about the rich?

A rich noble may have gone to a tournament. This was a series of competitions such as sword fighting, jousting and horseriding. There would be prizes for the best competitors. Rich men might also go hunting, or enjoy feasting or dancing. A group of acrobats or jugglers might entertain him and his guests. And if they got bored with the entertainers, they might play chess, draughts, cards, or throw dice.

In the Middle Ages a popular game for rich men was real tennis. Two players had to hit a wooden ball over a rope with a racquet. Sometimes the ball was hit so hard that players could be killed if it hit them on the head!

Do it yourself...

Whether you were rich or poor, you had to make your own fun in the Middle Ages. There were no cinemas or theatres to visit. You couldn't even go to an organized, professional sports match. But people must have enjoyed their spare time because they didn't get much of it. Holy days were rare, so ordinary people made sure that they made the most of them.

Archery
England's armies always needed archers. Boys had to practise from a very young age.

Stoolball
A young lady would sit on a stool and men would throw a ball at her. She would try to dodge the ball, perhaps using a bat to hit it away. If they hit her they got a kiss!

Bear baiting
A bear would be chained to a post while dogs attacked it. People would bet on the result – would the dogs or the bear win?

Wrestling
People loved all sorts of fighting games – the more blood the better.

Hungry for More?

Have you enjoyed any of the games or sports shown in the picture recently? If so, which ones? Have any of the sports or games changed at all? If so, how?

Be a Top Historian

These sports and pastimes are great examples of how some things from long ago **stay the same** whilst others **change** a lot… and there are always lots of reasons why some things change. For example, bear-baiting is no longer acceptable as it is considered cruel, whereas the game of conkers is largely unchanged because it is fun and easy to set up.

Work

1   Explain where the modern word 'holiday' comes from.

2   **a**   Look closely at the illustration showing ordinary people enjoying their holy day. Make two lists, one headed 'Things we no longer enjoy today' and the other headed 'Things we still enjoy today'.

   b   Choose one example from your list of things we no longer enjoy today. Explain why you think this pastime is no longer practised.

   c   Choose one example from your list of things we still enjoy today. Explain in what ways, if any, it has changed since medieval times.

3   Design a poster to advertise a medieval holy day in your town. Make sure you include the name of the holy day, a programme of events and fun activities taking place. Add some illustrations. Remember, all holy days began with a church service.

Has football changed much since the Middle Ages?

Over 1000 years ago, a small army from Denmark landed on the English coast and tried to steal as much as they could before sailing away again. However, their leader was captured and the angry English mob chopped off his head. The men then split into two groups and kicked the severed head around amongst each other. And this is how football in Britain began.

Mission Objectives

- Discover the origins of football in Britain.
- Evaluate how football in the Middle Ages differs from football today.

The game soon became known as 'mob football' when all the men from one village played another. They usually met up once or twice a year on public holidays such as Shrove Tuesday (Pancake Day). It was very violent. There could be as many as 500 players (including women sometimes), with few rules, no referee and the goals several miles apart. In Workington, an old rulebook said that players could use any method to get the ball to its target 'except murder'! The ball was a pig's bladder, stuffed with dried peas or sawdust. Sometimes a game was played with several balls!

'After lunch all the youth of the city go out into the fields to take part in the ball game. The students of each school have their own ball. The workers from each city craft also carry balls. Older citizens, fathers and wealthy men come on horseback to watch the juniors competing, and to revive their own youth. You can see their inner passions aroused as they watch the action and get caught up in the fun.'

▲ **SOURCE A:** *The first description of mob football played in London on Shrove Tuesday, written by William Fitzstephen in 1174.*

Hungry for More?

'Mob football' is still played in some parts of Britain today. Try to find out a bit more about this sport. Where is it played? Who plays it? How often? What are the rules? How do the players score?

SOURCE B: *A more modern view of football in the Middle Ages. A monk once described it as 'a devilish pastime. More a bloody murdering practice than a sport.'*

Banned

Football was regularly banned. In 1314, the Lord Mayor of London banned it: 'The hustling over large footballs causes great uproar in the city.' Despite the threat of imprisonment for anyone continuing to play, the ban was ignored! In 1331, King Edward III became the first king to officially ban football by royal decree. He said that people were playing it so much they were forgetting to practise their archery skills. The king was worried that if a foreign army invaded England, men would have forgotten how to use their bows and arrows properly.

Indeed, football was one of Britain's most banned games. Between 1314 and 1667, it was officially banned by more than 30 royal or local laws. Richard II, Henry IV and Henry V all tried to ban it, but people were so determined to play that they carried on regardless. In Scotland, King James I once famously ruled that 'na man play at the fute-ball', but the Scots loved the game so much they were playing football in Edinburgh the very next week.

FACT!

In 1321 the Pope issued a special letter of forgiveness to a player who had accidentally killed an opponent. A few days later a Londoner wrote that players used to 'retire home as from battle, with bloody heads, bones broken and out of joint and bruises that will shorten their days'. By 1450 players in some towns introduced a new rule to try to reduce the number of accidents: the ball could only be kicked, not carried or thrown.

SOURCE C: *A modern game of football. Can you spot any differences from mob football of the past?*

Work

1 a Write these statements in the correct chronological order.
   - A new rule was introduced in some towns saying the ball could only be kicked, not picked up.
   - King Edward III was the first king to ban football by royal decree.
   - A Danish prince's head was used as a ball.
   - The Pope issued a special letter to forgive a player who had killed an opponent.

   b Which of the above events do you think had the biggest effect on the game of football? Explain your answer.

2 a Make a list of all the differences you can find between football in the Middle Ages and football today.

   b What do you think the biggest difference is? Explain your answer.

3 a Why do you think so many kings tried to ban football?

   b Why do you think the bans weren't very successful?

Let me entertain you

The Middle Ages had its own pop songs and dance music. There was no recorded music or pop charts, but listening to a live band – and dancing around – were still very, very popular in medieval times. So what was medieval music like? Who performed this music? And what other types of entertainment were popular?

Music and dance

There were two types of music – 'sacred' (played in the church) and 'house' (played in and around people's homes). Church music had no harmonies, just a single singer singing a tune – and not one you'd spend the rest of the day humming! The music played outside church was much livelier. A band consisting of anything up to a dozen people would play all sorts of high tempo music on lots of different instruments (see **Source A**). People danced in large circles and moved around clapping, spinning and jumping in time to the beat. Singing over a mug of ale outside your house or on the village green was a very popular pastime.

> *Sumer Is Icumen In*
> Summer has come in,
> Loudly sing, Cuckoo!
> The seed grows and the meadow blooms
> And the wood springs anew,
> Sing, Cuckoo!
> The ewe bleats after the lamb
> The cow lows after the calf.
> The bullock stirs, the stag farts,
> Merrily sing, Cuckoo!

▲ **SOURCE B:** *A popular song from the thirteenth century. This was a bit like a pop song of today and was often sung in summer when the crops were growing well.*

SOURCE A: *Common instruments during the Middle Ages; as you can see, most were either string or wind instruments and many are still played today! Since there was no way of recording, all music was performed live.*

Wandering minstrels

Listening to musical instruments wasn't the only way to hear music. Singers known as **minstrels** wandered from town to town entertaining the crowds. They sometimes sang for the lord in his castle, if invited, but generally played out on the streets so people could dance and sing along. They would usually expect a few coins in return for their performance. However, the minstrels weren't just popular for their singing – often the news they brought from other parts of the country was just as interesting as the show. After all, wandering around so much meant that they knew all the gossip from the local towns and villages!

Play time

Plays were another popular form of live entertainment and drew large crowds. Originally, they were put on in church to teach peasants about the Bible or about saints. Over time, they became morality tales where good overcame evil, and were so popular they were moved outside. They were called **miracle plays** and were usually performed by groups of travelling actors who toured the country. Records show that plays were performed in 127 different towns during the Middle Ages and they must have been watched and enjoyed by thousands.

Wise Up Words

minstrel   miracle play

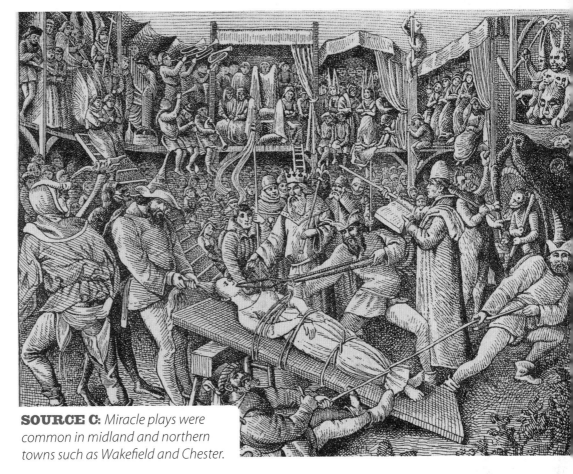

SOURCE C: *Miracle plays were common in midland and northern towns such as Wakefield and Chester.*

Work

1 a What is the difference between 'sacred' and 'house' music?

 b Which do you think was the more popular? Give reasons for your answer.

 c Why do you think music and plays were so important and popular in medieval Britain? Explain your answer carefully.

2 Look at **Source A**.

 a List which instruments you have heard of before. Have you played any of them?

 b Why was all music played live in the Middle Ages?

3 a What was a 'wandering minstrel'?

 b Apart from entertaining the crowds with music, what other role did wandering minstrels perform?

4 Read **Source B**.

 a Why do you think people in the Middle Ages enjoyed singing this song?

 b Do you think songs about cuckoos and farm animals would be good topics for a pop song today? Explain your answer.

5 Look at **Source C**. What was a 'miracle play'?

Keeping in fashion

To many people today, fashion is very important. You only have to look in any newsagents to see dozens of fashion magazines, and whole satellite channels are dedicated to following the latest trends. Most of you reading this page right now will be aware of the newest trends in shoes, hairstyles and jewellery.

Mission Objectives

- Understand the role fashion played in the lives of the rich and how fashion changed during the Middle Ages.

Dress to impress

Fashion was important in the Middle Ages too. The rich dressed in fancy clothes to impress each other. Clothes became a status symbol, with lords and ladies trying to outdo each other by wearing the latest costumes made from fine wool, leather, linen, velvet, silk, or fur. They decorated these clothes with gold and silver thread, jewels, chains, and fancy buttons. Even the coloured cloth used to make the clothes had different meanings: red meant you were in love, yellow meant anger and grey meant sadness. Natural dyes (made from plants, berries, nuts, crushed insects, and even rust) were used to make the different coloured cloth.

Female fashion
Women's dresses were always long and got brighter and more elaborate throughout the Middle Ages.

late Saxon   1300s   1400s

Hats

Women often hid their hair beneath fancy hats, some shaped like animal horns or butterfly wings. The famous 'steeple hat', which was cone shaped and very fashionable in the late 1480s, was nearly a metre tall.

1300 → 1350 → 1400 → 1400

1400 → 1420 → 1450 → 1480

Following fashion

In the early Middle Ages, the rich wore fairly simple clothes – but as the years passed, fashions became more and more elaborate. Dresses got longer, hats got taller, cloth got brighter, and shoes got pointier. And just like today, hats, shoes, hairstyles, coats, dresses, and cloaks varied from year to year, so it was a constant fight for the most dedicated followers of fashion to keep ahead.

Shoes
Pointed shoes called 'poulaines' were very fashionable in the Middle Ages. In fact, some shoes were so pointed that the toes had to be tied back. And platform shoes called 'pattens' were common too, for walking through the filthy, muddy streets.

Male fashion
A well-dressed nobleman might wear a tunic, leggings and a hat, but throughout the Middle Ages the style of hat, length of tunic, thickness of robes, and tightness of leggings varied.

1100 → 1350 → 1470

Did peasants follow fashion?

It was a very different story for the ordinary peasants. Following the latest fashions meant nothing to them. Instead, they wore plain and simple tunics, woollen leggings, straw or woollen hats, hoods, and capes. They dressed in dull colours such as grey, brown and dark green. Some peasants couldn't even afford to buy shoes. Their clothes were nearly always handmade and would last for years!

Peasants' clothes
Peasants' clothes were made from coarse wool or linen. They dressed practically rather than fashionably. In winter they kept warm by wearing leather or sheepskin jackets.

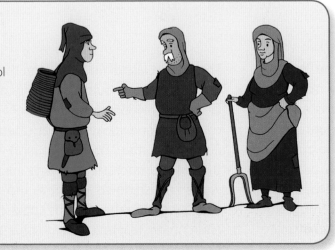

Work

1 a Why was fashion so important to rich people in the Middle Ages?

 b How could the clothes a person wore express how they might be feeling?

 c In your own words, explain how and why a poor person's clothes differed from a rich person's.

2 **The Big Write!**

We all know that there were no fashion magazines in medieval England, but imagine that there were! Imagine you are an editor for a fashion magazine during the Middle Ages. You need to prepare a double-page spread for a magazine bought by the rich and fashionable. Your feature could include the following:

· latest fashions
· fashion dos and don'ts
· what the best-dressed people are wearing
· the key points about the fashions, for example, how pointed your hat should be
· a 'headline' or spread title – this needs to be catchy and encourage the reader to do more than glance at your article
· examples of fashion styles
· bright, clear, colourful pictures
· a layout like a magazine – look at examples in current magazines to help you.

The story of the English language

In medieval Britain, several languages were spoken including, among others, Welsh in Wales and Gaelic in Scotland. And what was the main language in England? English, of course. But did you know that for many years after 1066, it was the third most important language in England? So how did the English language survive? Why had it become less important after 1066? What did English sound like during this time? And how did English develop and become the number one language in England by the end of the Middle Ages?

Mission Objectives

- Investigate the origins of the main language spoken in Britain today.

Before 1066...

Before William the Conqueror and his men invaded (and took over) in 1066, the people of England spoke a language called Old English. This was a mixture of different languages taken from the various peoples who had invaded England over the years (see **Source A**).

Norse: From the 700s onwards, the Vikings attacked and settled in England. These 'Norse men', as they were sometimes called, added some of their own words to Old English. Many of the words they introduced were connected with place names, such as 'by' which is Norse for a settlement. As a result, we get Grimsby and Whitby. Sometimes the Vikings settled in a village, and Norse for a village is 'thorpe', so we get Scunthorpe and Cleethorpes. Other Viking or Norse words include anger, build, dregs, flit, gate, glitter, oaf, neck, skin, ugly, and you.

Latin: When Britain became a Christian land, a number of Latin words (mainly connected with the Church) came into use. Some Latin words that still survive today are bishop, church and monk. Other Latin words or phrases such as alter ego, factor, parent and et cetera (although we write 'etc.' today) are still used frequently.

Anglo-Saxon: Tribes called Angles, Saxons and Jutes from Germany and Denmark invaded Britain about 1500 years ago. The Anglo-Saxons were great storytellers. The language they spoke would be difficult for us to understand but some of their words still survive. Indeed, if you could travel back in time and speak to an Anglo-Saxon you would really struggle to know what he was talking about, but you might be able to understand some words such as drink, father, ground, love, name, silly, son, the, was, and wife.

NORSE

LATIN

ANGLO-SAXON

SOURCE A:
Old English was influenced by three main languages.

OLD ENGLISH

After 1066...

In 1066, William the Conqueror brought the French language to England and King Harold, the man he had defeated at Hastings, was the last Old English-speaking king! All the important people William brought over from France spoke French like himself – the queen, the barons, their wives and their children. They brought new French words with them too – words that we still know today, such as archer, army, arrest, baron, battle, castle, city, enemy, grape, guard, judge, market, plate, prison, sausage, sugar, and traitor.

The ruling class of England (and their lawyers, priests and secretaries) could also speak Latin – a living language in 1066. Latin was taught in schools and cathedrals and spoken by educated people all over Europe. So, after 1066, Old English was officially the third most important language in England. Nobody wrote English down any more and nobody seemed to care! Kings and their friends spoke French (and Latin); churchmen, teachers and merchants used Latin, and books were even written in Latin too.

English survives

But Old English didn't die out because ordinary peasants and townspeople spoke it every day. They wouldn't and couldn't learn French or Latin, so they kept on speaking the language they had known all their lives – Old English!

In the mix

However, as the centuries passed, Old English and French began to mix (just as the people did). An Old English-speaking peasant who knew a worker up at the castle might use a French word; a French nobleman visiting the local town would also use a French word. He then might visit another town, pick up a few Old English words and use them with his friends. Latin was still the language of the Church, but in trade, business and the growing towns and villages, it was awkward to have different languages, so they gradually blended into one. By the 1400s, something very similar to modern English had emerged.

Arabic	admiral; alcohol; sofa
Japanese	judo; sushi; tycoon
Inuit	anorak; igloo; kayak
Turkish	coffee; yoghurt
Czech	pistol; robot
Welsh	corgi; flannel
Portuguese	albatross; marmalade; palaver
Norwegian	ski; slalom
Hungarian	coach; goulash; paprika
Scottish Gaelic	slogan; trousers
Aztec	chilli; chocolate; tomato
Russian	mammoth; vodka

▲ **SOURCE C:** *The English language continues to absorb words from all over the world. This list gives just a few everyday words from other languages.*

'Chaucer has often been referred to as the "saviour of the English language". As a writer of the famous "Canterbury Tales", he wrote mainly in English, the language of ordinary people, but used French words when he didn't think an English one fitted. For example, instead of using the word "hard" (Old English) he may choose the word "difficult" (French). He thought his writing was improved by the richness of the English language. He had so many words to choose from – Old English, French, Latin, Norse and Anglo-Saxon.'

▲ **SOURCE B:** *From a modern history book about Chaucer.*

SOURCE D: *This manuscript includes a picture of Chaucer, a famous writer from the Middle Ages.*

Work

1 **a** In your own words, explain what is meant by the term 'Old English'.
   b Why did French replace Old English as the dominant language in the Middle Ages?

2 Why do you think English eventually replaced French and Latin?

3 Look at **Source B**. According to this source, how was Chaucer helped by the variety of languages that had been used in England over the years?

4 **a** The English language is always changing. Think carefully and write down why you think the English language changes so much.
   b Make a list of words and phrases used today which your grandparents wouldn't understand. Try to explain why they wouldn't understand them.

FACT!

Many medieval kings spoke French, and couldn't read or write either! It was Edward III who realized that English, not French or Latin, was still spoken by millions of ordinary people and allowed English to be used in Parliament and in law courts. Soon after, Henry IV became the first monarch in over 300 years to make his first speech as a king in English.

Come dine with me!

Think about what you have eaten over the last week. You may find that you've eaten chocolate bars, a few burgers or pizzas, chicken nuggets or maybe something more healthy such as pasta, rice or fruit and vegetables grown locally or imported from abroad. Today, we have more choice in where we get all our food, what we eat, even how we cook it, than ever before. Things have certainly changed a lot since the Middle Ages. So what was it like to eat in medieval Britain?

It ain't pleasant for a peasant

A peasant's food was pretty dull and was the same year in, year out. There was no tea, coffee, orange juice, or fizzy drinks and the water wasn't usually fit to drink so they drank a watery kind of beer called **ale**. Look at **Source A** to see a typical peasant's diet.

Healthy diet

Peasants grew a lot of strong-flavoured vegetables and herbs to make their dull food tastier. Onions, garlic, leeks, cabbage, carrots, parsley, and mint were common. Apples, cherries, pears, and wild berries were also eaten (and sometimes made into fruit pies) and honey was one of the few ways to sweeten anything. In fact, a peasant's diet was probably much healthier than most people's today. They didn't eat food that contained large amounts of sugar (like cakes, biscuits and chocolate bars) and they worked all day so they got lots of exercise!

Breakfast: Bread and ale

4am to 6am

Dinner: Bread, cheese, onion, eggs, ale or cider

10am

Supper: Bread, fish, thick vegetable soup

4pm

SOURCE A: *A peasant's daily meals.*

What about the meat?

If peasants did eat meat, it was usually bacon. This was the most common meat amongst peasants because pigs were very easy to keep. However, they sometimes ate food that people today would find unusual – squirrel, hedgehog, pike, and eel, for example. There were no refrigerators to keep food fresh so meat was usually salted or smoked. Peasants would rub salt into meat to stop it going bad, or hang strips of meat from the roof of their cottage so it would dry out and last longer.

FACT!

Potatoes didn't reach England until the 1500s so there were no chips or potato wedges for the peasants to enjoy!

FACT!

Today, many people have a taste for salty or smoked food. For example, some of you will put extra salt on your chips or enjoy 'smoky bacon' crisps or 'smoked' kippers. We like these things because humans have been preserving food like this for thousands of years and our taste buds haven't changed much in that time.

Life in the manor house

For the richer folk, daily life was a lot easier than it was for the peasants. They had servants to do most things for them, including the cooking! They still ate a lot of bread, but it was of better quality. Like a peasant, a rich noble would eat three times a day, but would eat a lot more meat – and drink a lot more wine! Soups and stews were common, as were puddings, such as fruit tarts or pancakes.

Medieval feast

For a special occasion, the lord and lady of the manor would hold a feast in their largest room – the great hall. A servant would lay out spoons, knives, drinking cups, and bread. Forks were rare. The lord and his guests would probably have spent the day hunting for the meat about to be eaten – venison (deer), wild boar, ducks, swans, or even peacocks. Slices of stale bread called **trenchers** were used as plates. The juices from the meat and vegetables would soak into them and when the meal was over they might be given to the poor – or thrown to the dogs (see **Source B**). Servants would then carry around warm bowls of water and bits of cloth so that guests could rinse and clean their fingers after eating.

SOURCE B: *A medieval feast. Can you see*
i) the servants
ii) the dog eating from the table
iii) the man begging for food
iv) the entertainers?

Work

1   Copy out and complete this paragraph, choosing one answer from the bold words in the brackets.

A peasant's basic food was (**bread/ potatoes**) which he ate with all meals. Cheese, eggs and fish were popular too. They drank (**lemonade/ale**) with most meals because the (**water/whisky**) was not fit to drink. Peasants often had a small (**garden/garage**) next to their cottage where they grew lots of strong-flavoured (**fruits/ vegetables**) and herbs to make their dull food a bit (**more dull/ tastier**). (**Bacon/Lamb**) was one of the most common meats because (**dogs/pigs**) were so easy to keep. To preserve food over the long winter months, meat and fish were (**frozen/salted/tinned**) and smoked.

2   **a**   Copy out the diagram of a peasant's meals (**Source A**).
    b   Now draw a similar diagram to show your meals during one of the days in the last week. Remember to include everything you have eaten, even snacks.
    c   Write down at least two ways in which the peasant's meals are different from your meals. Then make a judgement – which diet is healthier? Yours or theirs?

3   Look at **Source B**.
    a   Describe what's going on in the picture in as much detail as you can.
    b   Produce a menu for a medieval feast like this one. Try to include lots of food. Remember, most people couldn't read, so you'll need to illustrate your menu.

Mission Objectives

- Consider the role of the knight in medieval society.
- Judge whether aspects of medieval history still have relevance today.

Have you ever shaken hands with your opponent before and after a football match? Or have you given up your seat on a bus for an elderly person or pregnant woman? Have you ever held a door open for someone, or allowed them to go through the door before you? If the answer to any of these questions is 'yes', you have probably been told what good manners you have. The person you've helped knows you didn't have to do any of these things, but they (and you) feel much better for it. So why do we do this? Where does this sort of behaviour come from?

From the Middle Ages?

Lots of sports today include these ideas about behaving properly and being courteous. For example, when playing golf or snooker, there are no rules to stop you making a noise when your opponent is taking a shot, but players are quiet when their opponent is playing. This is because they don't want to distract them and be seen as unsporting. But this idea of behaving in the correct manner comes from the Middle Ages. And it all started with the best warriors in Europe – the knights.

The knight's code

The first knights were just soldiers on horseback. William the Conqueror brought them to England in 1066 to fight King Harold. As a reward for beating Harold, King William gave them land. In return, they promised to spend 40 days a year fighting for their king. This was called **paying homage**. From the twelfth century onwards, though, knights were expected to follow a strict code of honour, called **chivalry**. Inspired by Christian teachings, chivalry demanded that knights were kind, truthful, loyal, polite, and brave in battle. They had to spend money and choose friends wisely, never break a promise and defend people who couldn't defend themselves.

The 'Code of Chivalry' also stated that the knights had to treat women especially well. They should fight for a woman, do brave things for her, and even write her poems! Even today, when a man helps out a woman in an extra special or kind way, it is often said that 'he was like a knight in shining armour!' Over the years, this idea of behaving correctly and considerately was passed down and still survives today. So next time someone thanks you for giving up your seat for them or holding open a door, just say, 'It's OK, I'm just being chivalrous!'

So how did you become a knight?

If you wanted to be a knight, having a rich father helped. Being a knight was expensive because you had to pay for all your horses and weapons – and you were expected to give expensive gifts to your friends.

A knight's training would start at seven years of age when he would be sent to a knight's home to serve him. The **page**, as the boy would be known, would clean dishes, serve meals and wash clothes, and might learn to read and write. At about 14 years old, the page would become a **squire**. He would learn about chivalry, weapons, fighting, armour, and horses. And if the squire worked hard enough for another seven years, he might be ready to become a full knight. The cartoons on the next page show the ceremony a young man would eventually go through to become a knight.

SOURCE A:
Re-enactments of medieval tournaments are popular tourist attractions, and regularly take place at castles in Britain during the summer holidays.

A knight at last!

1 The young squire has waited years for this. He has learned all there is to know about being a knight, and now his time has arrived!

2 The night before, he has a bath to wash away his sins.

3 Then he spends the night in church praying. He promises to be a good and worthy knight. The white tunic shows he is pure; the red robe means he is prepared to spill blood for his king.

4 Helped by the page and another squire, he puts on all his armour ready for the knighting ceremony.

Arise!

5 The squire kneels before his lord, or even the king, and promises to be loyal and brave and to protect the poor and weak. He is then 'dubbed' (touched) on each shoulder with the flat of his own sword.

6 A knight is born! He is often presented with a set of spurs (used to control a horse), a sword and a new suit of armour. The priest will bless him so he should always triumph in battle. He is also usually given land and reminded that he must spend 40 days a year fighting for his lord.

Work

1 Explain the following words and phrases: chivalry; paying homage; dubbed.

2 What is the difference between a page and a squire?

3 Make a list of five things that people do today that could belong to a modern code of chivalry.

4 In pairs or small groups, write a code of chivalry for your classroom or school. Think it through carefully. You could put it on display and try to follow it.

Welcome to the tournament

If there wasn't a war to keep a knight fit and his skills sharp, the next best thing was a **tournament**. This was a big, organized series of competitions – and a fun day out for visitors and spectators. It also gave a knight the chance to become rich and win prizes.

Mission Objectives

- Explain why tournaments took place.
- Investigate what different activities took place in a medieval tournament.

So much to see!

Look at the picture of a tournament and identify all the different events and entertainment that took place.

1   Tents for visiting knights.

2   An archery competition taking place.

3   The tournament **marshal**. He was like a referee, making sure that everyone followed the rules and didn't cheat.

4   A joust taking place. Knights on horseback would ride at each other and try to hit their opponent with a three metre long **lance**. Three points were awarded if a knight knocked his opponent off his horse, two points if he hit him on the head and one point if he hit any other part of his body. A point would be lost if he hit the horse. Also, if a knight fell off his horse, the opponent got to keep his armour and horse.

5   The **herald** announced the names of the knights in each contest.

6   The coats of arms of each knight taking part in the tournament.

7   A sword fighting competition. Not all knights jousted – some preferred other tournament games.

8   The ale tent.

9   A poor beggar, hoping that some of the crowd will take pity on him and throw him a few coins.

10   Entertainers performing for the crowd.

11   A stand for spectators.

12   The local lord and lady who were hosting the tournament.

13   Dog fighting – people would bet on the result.

14 A beaten knight trying to buy back the horse he lost for falling off during the joust.

15 Winner's prize. Often this was a golden cup or a silver plate, but sometimes the prizes were rather unusual – in London in 1216 the prize was a huge brown bear! Some knights made a living out of jousting, taking part in tournaments all over Europe.

16 An injured knight. Although the competitions were not designed to hurt the knights, injuries were common – so were deaths!

17 A dancing bear – people would pay to watch this.

18 The **tilt**. This barrier was introduced to stop the knight who has been knocked off his horse being trampled to death by his opponent's horse.

Wise Up Words

herald   lance   marshal
tilt   tournament

19 Lance – these weren't sharp because the knights weren't trying to kill each other.

20 Knights waiting to joust.

21 Horses were protected with armour and padding.

22 A grandstand for the richest and most important guests.

Work

1 What is the difference between a marshal and a herald?

2 Why do you think tournaments were so popular among:
   a knights
   b spectators?

3 What was jousting? Make sure you explain the points system in your answer.

4 Re-enactments of medieval tournaments are a popular tourist attraction today. They regularly take place at castles in school holidays. Some of you might have seen one! Imagine you are designing a poster or flyer for a modern re-enactment of a medieval tournament. Outline what people will see. How would you attract people? What could you charge for entry? What explanations might you need to add to your poster to help people understand what they're coming to see?

What was heraldry?

Once a knight put on his armour, he looked the same as any other knight. So, in order to stand out when jousting in tournaments, or to avoid being killed by his own men during battle, the knight decorated his shield. The designs were made up of special pictures, patterns or colours. This special design was known as a **coat of arms**. Sometimes the knight would also wear a tunic or carry a flag with the same design as his shield. A coat of arms was a knight's personal badge and had to be easy to recognize. After all, during battle it was vital to know instantly who was coming towards you so you knew which side he was on. As the years went by, the patterns became very complicated and complex rules for their creation, called **heraldry**, were developed.

Mission Objectives

- Analyse the rules of heraldry.
- Explain why heraldry was important in medieval society.

Rules of heraldry

When designing his coat of arms, a knight had to follow several strict rules. To begin with, a knight was only allowed to use five basic colours – purple, blue, red, black, and green. He was also allowed to use two metal colours – gold and silver. A knight then had to choose a simple design (see **Source A**).

There were even strict rules when selecting the colours for a pattern. For example, you couldn't put a metal next to a metal or a colour next to a colour (see **Source B**).

Wise Up Words

coat of arms   heraldry

SOURCE A: *Each basic pattern had its own name.*

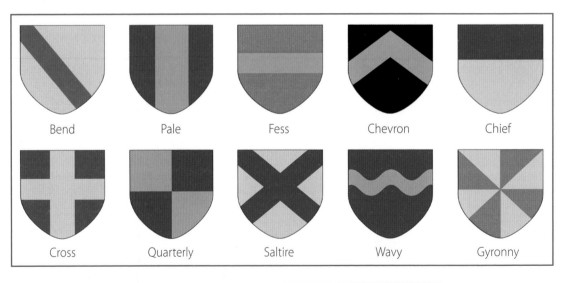

Bend   Pale   Fess   Chevron   Chief

Cross   Quarterly   Saltire   Wavy   Gyronny

Armour

A suit of armour could cost up to £75,000 in today's money. Most suits looked the same, so a distinctive coat of arms was very important in order to tell the knights apart.

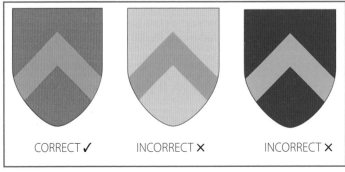

CORRECT ✓   INCORRECT ✗   INCORRECT ✗

SOURCE B: *Colour rules for a knight's coat of arms.*

Choosing your charge

A coat of arms often had a 'charge' – an image that represented something about the knight or his family (see below).

strength and protection	safety and trust	strength and alertness	faithfulness	courage	a good judge
wisdom	ready for anything	bravery	beauty	truth	affection

SOURCE D: *This illustration from the 1400s shows a knight in coat of arms.*

Family matters

Coats of arms were passed down through the generations and became family badges. They were used on everything – walls, gates, flags, clothes, windows, even plates and cutlery. When the members of two important families married, their coats of arms were joined, and if they had children, special symbols were used that indicated their rank within the family (see **Source C**).

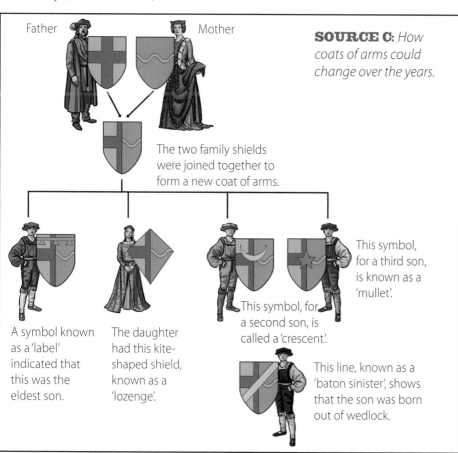

SOURCE C: *How coats of arms could change over the years.*

Father   Mother

The two family shields were joined together to form a new coat of arms.

A symbol known as a 'label' indicated that this was the eldest son.

The daughter had this kite-shaped shield, known as a 'lozenge'.

This symbol, for a second son, is called a 'crescent'.

This symbol, for a third son, is known as a 'mullet'.

This line, known as a 'baton sinister', shows that the son was born out of wedlock.

Work

1 In heraldry, what was:
   a a pattern?
   b a charge?

2 In your own words, explain the rules about colours and metals that knights had to follow when designing their coat of arms.

3 Why was a coat of arms important for a knight?

4 Design your own coat of arms. Choose the basic pattern, charges and colour – and remember to stick to the colours and metals rule! Then write a paragraph explaining the choices you made when designing it.

Men held nearly all the top jobs in the Middle Ages – kings, knights, lawyers, bishops, and even village officials. So what were the women up to? How were their lives different from those of women today? And, since half the medieval population was female, why aren't they mentioned more often?

Mission Objectives

- Compare the rights of women today with those of women in the Middle Ages.
- Explain why there was little written about the lives of women.

Second class citizens

In medieval Britain, women were seen as the possessions of men. In other words, they belonged to either their father or their husband. If women got into trouble, it would be their closest male relative who appeared in court, not the woman herself. Most people at the time believed that women were **inferior** to men – both physically and mentally. If a man felt that his wife was nagging too much or he thought she was getting too big for her boots, he could legally put her in a **scold's bridle** (see **Source A**). The bad news for women didn't end there; they were banned from lots of things we would now take for granted (see below).

SOURCE A:
An iron muzzle or cage, the scold's bridle had an iron gag which was pushed into the wearer's mouth making talking difficult or even painful.

A woman cannot:
- marry without her parents' permission;
- own property, clothes or jewellery – it belongs to her husband;
- divorce her husband – even if he beats her;
- train to be a doctor, lawyer, priest, or judge;
- go to a shop, inn or travel on her own;
- wear tight or revealing clothes;
- speak rudely.

Missing history

A lot of the information we have about the Middle Ages comes from monks. They made up one of the few groups that could read and write – and they didn't have a great deal to do with women! They wrote about things that interested them, such as religion, rulers and fights between countries. Women didn't have a great deal to do with these things and most monks had no contact with women, so they were hardly mentioned.

Village women

Ordinary women's lives were tough. Their only education came from their mothers and they learned how to cook, sew and care for children and animals. The average age for girls to marry was 17, although some brides were as young as 13! If the woman lived in the countryside, she would either work in the fields or make cloth at home. As well as working all day, she was expected to cook all the food and care for the children!

SOURCE B: *A woman's job was to look after the children and make sure food was prepared.*

Town women

It was possible for women to learn a trade in some of the bigger towns. The most common jobs for women were spinning and weaving cloth – unmarried women are still called spinsters today. Many women ran businesses but only after their husbands had died. Women couldn't start their own firms but they could inherit one.

Rich women

A girl from a wealthy family wouldn't have chosen her husband – her family would have done it for her. The husband received a **dowry**, a payment from his new wife's family, when he got married. Wealthy women had time for fun, which would usually involve dancing and music. Although they received less education than rich men, women were expected to run the family household and manage the servants.

SOURCE D: *This medieval picture shows women fighting. Although there weren't female soldiers, women helped defend castles in sieges when things got desperate.*

Wise Up Words

dowry   inferior   scold's bridle

SOURCE C: *This picture of hardworking women was drawn in about 1330.*

Work

1 **a** What is meant by the word 'inferior'?
   b Make a list of all the ways in which women were not treated as equal to men in medieval Britain.

2 Writing in full sentences and using capital letters and full stops, explain why historians don't know much about the lives of women in the Middle Ages.

3 **a** What is a dowry?
   b What advantages and disadvantages do you think choosing a husband for their daughter would bring a medieval family?

4 **Interview with…**
   Imagine you got to meet a woman from the Middle Ages. What three interview questions would you ask her? And, what three pieces of information would you share with her about the role of women today?

Matilda: the forgotten queen

Having seen how women were treated during the Middle Ages, it may not surprise you to learn that between 1066 and 1553 there were no female monarchs in England. Women were viewed as too weak to rule a whole country. In 1135, all that nearly changed when Princess Matilda was named as next in line to the throne. So why wasn't Matilda crowned queen? Who gained control of the country instead? How did she react? And who would have made the better ruler?

Mission Objectives

- Investigate why Matilda thought she should have been crowned queen in 1135.
- Explain the reasons why she wasn't.
- Judge who won in the struggle between Stephen and Matilda.

Henry's got no heir!

In 1120, King Henry I was the father of two sons and two daughters. He was certain that one of his children would rule after him. Then disaster struck! Both of his sons drowned coming back from France. It is said that after Henry heard the news, he never smiled again. But he was still desperate to ensure that the Crown remained in his family, so before he died he made all the important, powerful barons swear to make his daughter, Matilda, queen after he was gone. But the thought of having a woman in charge was too much for many of them. When Henry died, they broke their promise, and put the king's nephew, Stephen, on the throne. Look at the fact files for both Stephen and Matilda.

Matilda

Background: She married a German king when she was 12 years old and lived in Germany for ten years until her husband died in 1125. Henry I soon found another husband for her – and 26-year-old Matilda married a 14-year-old French prince! Despite the difference in ages and rumours that they didn't get on, the couple had three sons in four years.

Claim to the throne: She was the eldest child of Henry I and was her father's choice as heir. The barons had sworn to make her queen.

Personality: She grew up in Germany and didn't seem to like England much. She could be rude and didn't make friends easily.

Stephen

Background: His father had been killed fighting abroad when Stephen was just five years old. He was brought up by his uncle, Henry I, and soon became a great favourite of the king. He was given huge amounts of land by Henry, and by the time the king died, Stephen was the richest man in England.

Claim to the throne: Despite swearing to support his cousin Matilda, Stephen didn't think a woman was capable of controlling England. As he was one of Henry's closest male relatives, Stephen decided that the Crown should be his!

Personality: He was very mild-mannered and good tempered. He was sometimes accused of being too laid back.

So what happened?

1 When King Henry I died in 1135, Stephen raced to London and was crowned king. But he was weak and his supporters took advantage of him. Soon the country was in chaos and people starved.

2 But soon Matilda began to increase her support. There was fierce fighting between both sides. Eventually, Matilda's forces captured Stephen and she declared herself 'Lady of the English'.

3 But Matilda's victory didn't last long. The people of London didn't like her and rose up against her. She had to flee to France for safety… and Stephen became king again!

4 Matilda didn't give up, and after more fighting Stephen and Matilda reached a deal. She agreed to stop fighting if *her* son (Henry) and neither of Stephen's sons (Eustace and William) could be king after Stephen's death. So when Stephen died in 1154, it was Matilda's son who became King Henry II.

> 'In the days of this king [Stephen], there was nothing but strife, evil and robbery, for quickly the great men rose against him. When the traitors saw that Stephen was a good humoured, kindly man who inflicted no punishment, they committed all manner of horrible crimes. Every powerful man built himself castles and held them against the king. It grew worse and worse. They took tax, as protection money, from villages. When the wretched people had no more to give, they robbed and burned all the villages.'

▲ **SOURCE A:** *A description of the way the barons took control when Stephen was on the throne, written in a monk's chronicle.*

> 'Matilda sent for the richest men and demanded from them a huge sum of money, not with gentleness but with the voice of authority. They complained they did not have any money left. When the people said this, Matilda, with a very grim look, every trace of a woman's gentleness removed from her face, blazed into unbearable fury.'

▲ **SOURCE B:** *A description of Matilda written when she was in control of the country.*

Work

1 a Why didn't one of Henry I's sons become king in 1135?
   b Why do you think Henry I named Matilda and not Stephen as heir to England's throne?
   c Find as many reasons as you can that explain why Matilda wasn't made queen in 1135.

2 Look at **Source A**.
   a What, according to this source, happened in England under Stephen's rule?
   b In what ways does this source criticize Stephen?

3 a Look at **Source B**. In what ways, according to this source, was Matilda different from Stephen?
   b The man who wrote this source supported Stephen and not Matilda. How might knowing this affect how you view what the writer says about her?

4 Imagine a children's television programme has asked you to prepare a one-minute feature on Matilda. What would you say about her? What could the feature be called? What images would you include? What would you say about Stephen? Write a script for your feature.

Crown versus Church: the story of Henry II and Thomas Becket

We all know that kings and queens were very powerful and important people in medieval times. But did they *always* get their own way? The next few pages look at a well-known occasion in the Middle Ages when a king's power was tested... and which led to a vicious murder inside one of Britain's most famous cathedrals.

Mission Objectives

- Summarize the events in the quarrel between Henry II and Becket in the correct chronological order.
- Evaluate King Henry's motives in making Becket Archbishop of Canterbury.

Best of friends

In 1154, Henry II became King of England. One of his best friends was a man called Thomas Becket. They hunted and got drunk together. They both enjoyed expensive clothes, magnificent palaces and the very best food and wine. Henry respected and trusted Thomas so much that he made him **Chancellor**. This was a very important job and meant he was in charge of the country when Henry was away.

Henry the hot head!

King Henry was a popular ruler but he did have one major fault – his temper. He liked to get his own way and, when he got angry, his eyes went bloodshot and he threw a massive tantrum. He once got so angry that he ripped all his clothes off, threw himself on the floor and started chewing pieces of straw!

Henry's master plan!

Despite being king, Henry did not have the power to punish everyone in his kingdom. People who worked for the Church and broke the law went to the Church's own courts instead, and this annoyed Henry. You may not think this was much of a problem but, at this time, one in six people worked for the Church in some way. Henry was worried that there was too much crime and he thought that the Church courts were too soft on lawbreakers. For example, the king's courts might cut off the hands of a thief, but the Church's courts would probably fine them. Henry wanted a clever and trusted friend he could put in charge of the Church. That way, the Church's courts would punish people the way he wanted – and his power would be complete!

Archbishop Becket

In 1162, Henry made his friend Thomas Becket the Archbishop of Canterbury, placing him in charge of religion in England. Becket would be based at Canterbury Cathedral in Kent. Unfortunately for the king, though, Becket took his new job very seriously indeed. He stopped getting drunk and wearing fancy clothes. He started to wear an itchy, goat-hair shirt and slept on the hard stone floor. Religion became very important to Becket and he spent hours praying every day. When Henry spoke to him about making changes to the Church courts, Becket refused. The two men began to argue, and after Henry lost his temper in one particularly nasty disagreement, Becket fled to France – for six years!

Guess who's Beck?

Becket eventually returned to Britain and the two men agreed to try and work together. But as soon as Becket returned it all kicked off again! Becket **excommunicated** all of the bishops who had helped Henry run Church business while he was away. This meant that they were sacked from their jobs, and were told they'd go straight to hell when they died!

When Henry found out, he was furious. In one of his rages he shouted, 'Is there no one who will rid me of this troublesome priest?' Four knights were standing nearby while the king ranted and raved. They decided that they could rid their king of this priest, and set off to Canterbury without delay.

Wise Up Words

Chancellor   excommunicated

Work

1 Before the four knights set out to kill Becket, the following events occurred. Write these down in the correct chronological order.
   - Becket ran away to France for six years.
   - Henry and Becket became best friends.
   - Henry made Becket Archbishop of Canterbury.
   - Henry made Becket Chancellor of England.
   - Henry was heard to say, 'Is there no one who will rid me of this troublesome priest?'
   - Becket excommunicated some bishops.

2 a Think of five adjectives to describe King Henry II.
   b Think of five adjectives to describe Thomas Becket.
   c Are any of your words the same? Using the words you have listed, write two paragraphs describing Henry and Becket.

3 Explain Henry's plan when he made Becket Archbishop of Canterbury. What went wrong with this plan?

What Happened When?

In 1154, the same year that Henry II became king, Birmingham and its 'Bullring' were founded. Also, the only English man ever to be Pope – Nicholas Breakspear – was chosen for the role in this year.

Newsflash: murder in the cathedral

The afternoon of 29 December 1170 was a dark and stormy one. Four knights, in full armour, had arrived outside Canterbury Cathedral. Some monks, sensing trouble, hurried inside to find Archbishop Becket and rush him to safety. The events that followed caused a sensation throughout medieval Europe. If it had happened today, it would have been a huge news story covered by lots of television channels and journalists. If there had been TV news in 1170 (which there wasn't – obviously!) it may have been presented something like this…

Mission Objectives

- Discover how Thomas Becket was murdered and by whom.
- Investigate the consequences of the murder.

TV newsreader: We're sorry to interrupt your scheduled programming, but amazing news has just come in. Thomas Becket, Archbishop of Canterbury, has been found dead at Canterbury Cathedral. Over to Annette Ball, our reporter, live at the scene.

TV reporter: I can confirm the news that Thomas Becket, the man in charge of religion in England, has been hacked to death inside the most important cathedral in the country. I can also exclusively reveal that the four men who have been officially linked with the murder are knights and were apparently acting under orders from King Henry! The knights, named as Reginald Fitzurse, William de Tracy, Richard Brito, and Hugh de Morville, have fled into the stormy night. But if it is confirmed that they are Henry's men, it will be the most sensational story of the century!

TV newsreader: Were there any witnesses?

TV reporter: I do have an eyewitness, Jill. His name is Edward Grim, a monk who claims to have seen it all. What can you tell us, Brother Edward?

Edward Grim (monk): It was truly awful, you'll have to forgive me – I'm still shaking with anger and fear. The murderers entered this house of God in full armour and with their swords drawn. Some of my brother monks had tried to bolt the doors to keep the knights out, but the Archbishop ordered them to be re-opened. He said, 'It's not right to make a fortress out of a house of prayer.'

In a crazed fury, one of the knights yelled out, 'Where is Thomas Becket, traitor to the king and country?'

Becket stood in front of his attackers and said, 'I am no traitor and I am ready to die.' The knights then grabbed hold of the Archbishop and tried to drag him outside in order to kill him. Becket clung to a pillar but, realizing that his time on earth was nearly over, he bowed his head in prayer and made his peace with God.

This was too much for the murderous knights and a sword was brought crashing down on Becket's head, nearly chopping my arm off as it passed. Then another sword slashed down, again at his head, but still Becket stood firm in his prayers. The third blow was swung with such force that it knocked the Archbishop to his knees.

As he knelt on the floor, a fourth and final blow cut off the top of his head – the sword of the murderer smashing to pieces on the cathedral floor with the force of the strike.

But these evil men weren't finished yet. One knight put his foot on the holy priest's neck and scattered his blood and brains all over the floor. I couldn't bear to look any more but Brother William said he saw one of them scooping Becket's brains out of his skull with his sword. The last thing I heard was one of the knights saying, 'Let us away, this fellow will get up no more!' With that, the murderers disappeared into the night.

TV reporter: Incredible scenes, Jill. This news will shock the country. People are already dipping rags in Becket's blood. King Henry II is yet to release a statement but we are standing by to get his reactions to this shocking story! Back to you in the studio.

TV reporter: That's the big question tonight. The knights claimed to be acting on King Henry's orders, but how will the king respond?

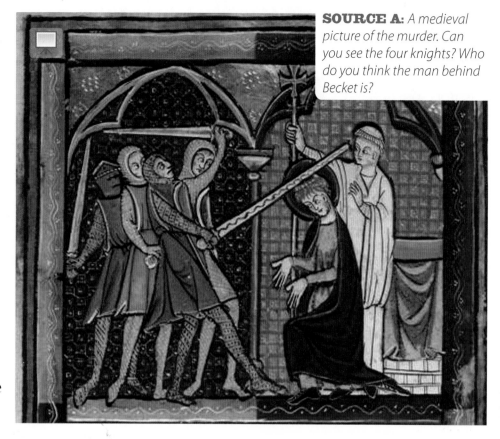

SOURCE A: *A medieval picture of the murder. Can you see the four knights? Who do you think the man behind Becket is?*

National sensation

Although this TV report is imaginary, the events it describes are recorded in witness statements and other evidence available to historians. The people of England were indeed shocked by Becket's murder and wondered what was going to happen next.

SOURCE B: *This diagram gives a bird's eye view of the attack.*

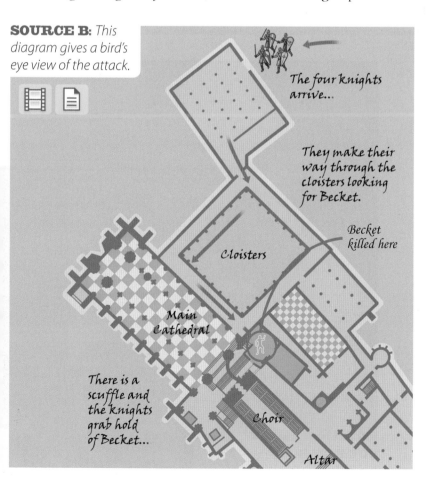

The four knights arrive...

They make their way through the cloisters looking for Becket.

Becket killed here

Cloisters

Main Cathedral

There is a scuffle and the knights grab hold of Becket...

Choir

Altar

Work

1 Why do you think the knights tried to drag Becket outside the cathedral?

2 Why do you think some people dipped rags in Becket's blood shortly after he was murdered?

SOURCE A: *Canterbury Cathedral in Kent was the scene of Becket's murder.*

How did Henry II react?

Henry was horrified when he heard the news. He hadn't exactly ordered the knights to go to Canterbury but he knew he was going to get the blame. He was terrified that he might be excommunicated by the Pope, the world leader of the Christian Church. So he decided to say sorry – in a big way! Henry walked the streets of Canterbury with no shoes on and, when his feet were cut and bleeding, he approached the cathedral. He then prayed at Becket's tomb while monks whipped his bare back. He spent the night on the hard stone floor – on the very spot where Becket was killed. It worked – the Pope forgave Henry.

SOURCE B: *An engraving of Henry II being whipped.*

What happened to the knights?

The knights were not as fortunate as Henry. They were sent on a pilgrimage – all the way to the Holy Land. None of them survived the long journey there.

Saint Thomas Becket

People started claiming miracles were taking place at Becket's tomb as soon as he died. Blind people claimed they could see and deaf people claimed they could hear after visiting his tomb. In 1173, Becket was made a saint by the Pope, and before long, the journey to pray at Becket's tomb was one of the most popular pilgrimages in Europe.

What Happened When? `1170`

In 1170, the same year that Becket is murdered, the Normans captured Dublin, Ireland.

SOURCE C: *People in the Middle Ages weren't so different from us in some ways! This is a lead badge that a pilgrim would have bought to show he had been to the tomb of Saint Thomas Becket. Have you ever bought a badge or other souvenir when you've visited somewhere special?*

Work

1 Who do you think was to blame for Becket's death? Find one reason to blame:
   - the knights
   - King Henry II
   - Becket himself.

   Overall, who do you blame most for the murder? Was it a combination of some or all of them? Explain your answer.

2 **The Big Write!**

   EITHER: Design a front page for a newspaper article reporting the events of 29 December 1170.

   Try to include the following details:
   - An eye-catching headline (can you use alliteration?)
   - the most important parts of the story in your first few sentences
   - Some quotes from an eyewitness
   - A picture of the crime scene
   - An interview with King Henry II

   OR: Imagine you are a town crier in 1170. These were people who stood in the centre of towns, ringing a bell and announcing the major news stories of the day. Write out how you would announce the death of Thomas Becket. Think about:
   - What one sentence would you say first to attract a crowd?
   - How will you make the story exciting and informative, and keep people listening?
   - How will you portray the king and Becket? Who will you support?
   - How will you end your amazing story?

   Your announcement should be no more than two minutes long.

3 Why do you think Henry reacted to Becket's murder the way he did?

4 Design a lead badge for pilgrims who visit Becket's tomb. Remember, it must have no words on it but must get the message across of where the pilgrim has been.

5 Who had the most power in medieval England – the Church or the Crown? Give reasons for your answer.

King John: Magna Carta man

The king's job was often complicated. It's true that kings lived a life of luxury, but they also had a job to do – they had to keep law and order, protect the country from attack, collect taxes, organize armies, and more! And sometimes kings made mistakes. They made poor decisions and upset or annoyed the people who helped them run the country. This double page investigates a king who made several mistakes… and explains how his actions changed the country forever.

Mission Objectives

- Analyse the consequences of King John's mistakes.
- Explain the importance of Magna Carta.

King John's struggles

King John was the son of Henry II and younger brother of King Richard. When his older brother died in 1199, John had little money left because Richard had spent so much of it fighting abroad! Unfortunately, King John soon did things that turned many people against him. The cartoon below sums up the main complaints of the barons and church leaders.

So what did the barons do?

By 1215 the barons had decided they'd had enough. They put together an army and marched towards London. Then they gave King John a choice – change the way he was running the country… or fight the army that was heading towards London!

King John gave in and asked the barons what they wanted. The barons made a list of 63 rights that they thought they should have. The main points are listed in **Source A**.

King John agrees

In June 1215, the barons met the king in a field at Runnymede, near Windsor, by the River Thames. After four days of discussions King John agreed to the list (known as 'Magna Carta')… and the barons agreed to be loyal to the king.

King John is a poor leader in battle. A few years ago, England ruled over lots of land in France… but not any more! The French have defeated us many times and regained much of their land as a result of John's mistakes.

We have even lost Normandy in France, the birthplace of William the Conqueror. I hear some people use the nickname 'Softsword' to describe King John!

And he keeps demanding higher and higher taxes to pay for battles he keeps losing! He has even started taxing sons when their fathers die! It's all money, money, money with King John!

King John has argued with the Pope many times. He made the Pope so angry that he closed all our churches for seven years. No one could get married or have a proper Christian burial.

John can be cruel too, or so I hear. He left the wife of one of his enemies to starve to death in prison. And he murdered his nephew in a drunken rage… apparently.

MAGNA CARTA 1215: THE MAIN BITS!

I, King John, accept that I have to run my country according to the law. I agree:

1. not to interfere with the Church
2. not to imprison nobles without a trial
3. that trials will be held quickly and fairly
4. to stop unfair taxes
5. not to ask for extra taxes
6. to let merchants travel around the country to buy and sell without having to pay large taxes.

SOURCE A: *'Magna Carta' means 'great charter'. King John never actually signed it because he couldn't write! So he stamped it with his royal seal to show he agreed.*

What happened next?

King John never liked the Magna Carta. He said he had been bullied into it. People accused the barons of being selfish too. After all, Magna Carta didn't apply to peasants, only to rich, important men like barons, knights and merchants.

However, as the years passed, Magna Carta became more and more important. It introduced the idea that there are certain laws and rules that even the king must accept… and that he couldn't do whatever he wanted. After King John died, other kings signed Magna Carta too, and today it is known as one of Britain's first steps on the road to becoming one of the most famous democracies in the world. In fact, some of the best-known parts of Magna Carta still apply to everyone today. For example:

- British people have the right to a fair trial before they can be punished.

- British people cannot be taxed unfairly.

Magna Carta

What Happened When? 1776

The Magna Carta inspired Americans when, in 1776, they began writing the rules by which their country is governed. They included: 'No person shall be held to answer for a crime without trial by jury nor shall their life, liberty or property be taken without following the law.'

Work

1 Think of three words that best describe King John. Say why you chose them.

2 Imagine you are a baron in England in 1214. Write King John a letter explaining why you're angry with him. Make sure you tell him what angers you most and why. Remember to set it out like a proper letter with the address of your castle and the king's address at the Tower of London at the top.

3 **a** Make a list of the main points in Magna Carta.
  b Which of the points are still important today?

4 **a** In a group, discuss the difference between 'short-term' and 'long-term'.
  b Was Magna Carta a short-term or a long-term success? Explain your answer.

5 Create your own Magna Carta for your school. List at least six changes you would like to see. These rules must apply to everybody – students and staff – and they must improve your school or education. Explain your reasons for each rule.

Kings had always asked rich, powerful landowners (called barons, earls, lords, and nobles) for advice on things like raising money or going to war. When kings met with advisors it was often called a **Great Council**. Sometimes there were arguments at these meetings… but the king nearly always got his own way!

This all changed in 1215 when King John ruled. The rich landowners rebelled and forced him to sign the Magna Carta, which said that the king couldn't do whatever he wanted! However, King John died in 1216 and his son became King Henry III when he was only nine years old. So what happened next? Would young Henry also agree to follow the rules laid down in Magna Carta… or would he just ignore them and rule however he wished? And how is all this linked to **Parliament** and the way Britain is ruled today?

Mission Objectives

- Examine why King Henry III argued with the barons.
- Discover the origins of Britain's Parliament.

The boy king

To begin with, young King Henry regularly met with the Great Council and took advice. But Henry didn't stay a boy forever – and when he got older, and got married, he began to ignore advice and ran things how he wanted. As you might imagine, this annoyed members of the Great Council. The cartoon below sums up their complaints.

And who's paying for all this? That's right – us! Our taxes go up because he spends so much.

Henry is spending a fortune on living a life of luxury. He even tried to buy the Italian island of Sicily as a present for his son!

And just like his father, he's not a very good soldier. He tried to take over large parts of France… and lost! And he expects us to provide soldiers and money for his expensive wars!

A Frenchman, Peter des Rivaux, has all the top jobs too. He's got over 20 jobs! In fact, Henry seems to give all the best jobs to his wife's friends and relatives.

And he's meddling with religion. Or rather, his wife is. She begged Henry to make her uncle – a Frenchman – the Archbishop of Canterbur[y]

He doesn't even take our advice any more. He just listens to his French wife and her French friends and relatives!

Enough is enough!

By 1258 the barons had had enough. They were fed up with high taxes and the fact that Henry listened more to his wife than to them. So the barons threatened to fight King Henry unless he agreed to meet up to discuss things. At a meeting in Oxford, the barons showed Henry a document called 'The Provisions of Oxford' (see **Source B**). As you can see by reading the document, if Henry agreed to this, the barons would have a lot more power… but Henry felt he had no choice – and signed it.

However, the king's son, 19-year-old Prince Edward, was furious that his father had been treated this way… and swore to get revenge!

Wise Up Words

Great Council   Parliament

SOURCE A: *This picture shows Henry III meeting with Parliament. By 1258 the barons were utterly fed up!*

Be a Top Historian

Top historians know that some things **develop slowly over time**. Parliament is a good example of how something that began in medieval times evolved over several centuries into the important body that it is today.

The Provisions of Oxford

- *The king cannot make decisions without the Great Council's agreement.*
- *The Great Council should choose the king's main advisors.*
- *A Parliament consisting of fifteen members of the Great Council, plus twelve other barons, has to meet at least three times a year.*

Signed,

Henry III and the Great Council

SOURCE B: *The Provisions of Oxford was signed in 1258. The word 'parliament' is from the French word 'parler', which means 'to talk'.*

Work

1 Write a sentence or two to explain the following terms:
   a Great Council
   b Provisions of Oxford

2 a Make a list of things that made Henry unpopular with his barons.
   b Which of these things do you think upset the barons the most? Make another list, putting them in order. Start with what you think annoyed the barons the most.
   c Can you connect the different problems in any way? Explain how some of them are linked.

SOURCE A: *The illustration shows the death of Simon de Montfort and is from the 1200s. It works a bit like a cartoon strip – first, de Montfort is stripped of his armour, then his body is cut to pieces. Later his head was sent to a man who hated him as a present!*

King Henry the prisoner

In 1264, King Henry III got an army together to fight the barons. He was unhappy that they'd made him sign the Provisions of Oxford because it took away a lot of his power. The king's army was led by Prince Edward, Henry's son. The baron's army was led by Simon de Montfort, who was married to King Henry's sister. On 14 May 1264, the two sides fought a battle at Lewes in Sussex. The barons won, and King Henry and Prince Edward were taken prisoner.

What happened next?

In 1265, Simon de Montfort called a meeting of the Great Council. But this time, he didn't just invite the rich, important bishops and barons. He also included two ordinary wealthy people from each large town and two knights from each county. This was the first time that ordinary people had been included in any sort of discussion about running the country. This meeting is often called 'the first Parliament'.

De Montfort is doomed!

Not surprisingly, the king and the young prince fought back. Prince Edward escaped from prison and gathered another army together. In August 1265, de Montfort's army was defeated at the Battle of Evesham. **Source A** shows the rather nasty way in which de Montfort was killed.

Parliament lives on

Although de Montfort died, his idea lived on. When Henry III died in 1272, Prince Edward became King Edward I. He didn't want to risk more fights with the barons by scrapping Parliament, so he kept meeting with them. Soon, the barons in Parliament realized that they were quite powerful. For example, if the king needed money (which he often did) he knew he couldn't go around collecting it all himself – he needed Parliament to get it for him. In return, Parliament could ask the king for permission to introduce new laws. So although Parliament couldn't exactly tell the king what to do, it was certainly a powerful force in the country because it controlled the king's money and could make new laws… just like today!

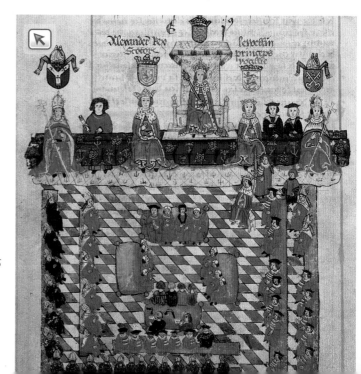

SOURCE B: *This picture wrongly shows rulers from Wales and Scotland at this Parliament. Llywelyn (Wales) and Alexander (Scotland) did not attend at the same time as King Edward.*

SOURCE C: *By the mid-1300s, meetings of Parliament had settled into a pattern that lasted for centuries. The British Parliament, made up of the House of Lords and the House of Commons, still meets like this today.*

The king

- *The king decided when Parliament was to meet, usually for a few weeks a year.*
- *Parliament couldn't stop collecting taxes for the king if they didn't like what he was doing.*

The Lords

- *Rich barons and bishops met in the House of Lords.*
- *The right to attend passed from father to son.*

The Commons

- *Voting took place in public. The men chosen were usually the richer people of the town and land-owning knights.*
- *These people became known as the 'commoners' or 'Commons' and met in the House of Commons.*

Work

1. Look at **Source A** on page 112 and **Source B** on this page. What are the main differences?

2. Explain the importance of the following dates in the development of Parliament:
   a 1264
   b 1265
   c 1272

3. a In what ways were each of the following men important in the development of Parliament?
      i   Simon de Montfort
      ii King Edward I

   b Which of the men do you think was the **most** important in the development of Parliament? Give reasons for your answer.

4. a How did Simon de Montfort die?
   b In what ways could de Montfort be seen as **both** a hero and a traitor?

5. What were the advantages of having a Parliament:
   a for the king?
   b for the barons, bishops, knights, and townspeople?

In today's world, large groups of people sometimes gather together because they are angry about something. They might hold a big meeting or march through the streets carrying banners and shouting slogans to express what they are unhappy about. When this happens it is called a **protest** and the people taking part are called **protesters**.

Mission Objectives

- Examine why peasants were so angry in 1381.
- Link some of the causes of the peasants' anger together.

You may have seen scenes like the one in **Source A** on news reports. Protests like this have taken place in recent years in Britain and in the rest of the world.

Hungry for More?

Can you think of any protests that have taken place recently? They could have taken place either in Britain or abroad. If so, do you know what the protest was about?

Sometimes, though, the protesters are so angry about things that they are prepared to use violence, which is illegal in today's society. Some protesters might get weapons and tell the leaders of a country to change things… or else! When this happens, it is usually called a **revolt** or a **rebellion**.

One of the best-known examples of rebellion in Britain happened during the summer of 1381. Ordinary people were so angry about the way they were forced to live that thousands of them marched to London, set fire to houses, murdered some of the king's men, and demanded that the king make changes to their lives. This event became known as the 'Peasants' Revolt'.

So why were the people so angry? Read some of the reasons for their anger on the next page.

SOURCE A: *This photo shows students protesting about tuition fees in London.*

There is a new tax called the Poll Tax. The king needs money to pay for his war with France and he wants 12 pence from everyone, rich and poor.

I don't own my own land — the local lord gives me some and I try to make a living from it by growing and selling crops. But I still have to work a few days a week for no wages. This is called 'work service' and I hate it. I just want to own my own land…

When we're not doing work service and actually get paid, our wages are very low. But it wasn't always like this! When the deadly disease called Black Death killed lots of workers, there were not enough people to do all the jobs. So we asked for more wages or else the work would not get done. For a time, our wages rose and rose. But then the king introduced a new law called 'Statute of Labourers' that said we couldn't earn more money than we did before the Black Death. It's not fair!

The rich can afford the taxes, but we can't. And they keep going up! We paid 4 pence in 1377… and now, in 1381, it's 12 pence!

Our king is only young. Richard II is 14 years old and is badly advised by greedy evil men who care only about making themselves rich… or so I've heard!

I have been very interested in what a priest called John Ball has been saying. He says that all men are equal in the eyes of God, and that this country won't be right until there is no difference between rich and poor.

What sparked the revolt?

On 30 May 1381, a group of King Richard's tax collectors arrived in the village of Fobbing in Essex to collect the hated Poll Tax money. The peasants refused to pay and attacked the tax collectors. Three of the king's men were killed but another escaped and rode back to London to tell the king. Soon, other tax collectors were attacked all over Essex and Kent. Before long, a large group of up to 60,000 angry peasants decided to march to London – the Peasants' Revolt had begun…

Wise Up Words

protest   protester
rebellion   revolt

Work

1. In your own words, explain what you think is meant by the following terms:
   a protest
   b protester
   c revolt
   d rebellion

2. Working in a small group, imagine that you all live in a village in Essex or Kent in May 1381. Your small group is determined to be part of the Peasants' Revolt… but some of your fellow villagers aren't so sure! Your task is to convince other people in your village to join the Peasants' Revolt and march to London with you.

   a Prepare a short speech outlining your reasons for taking part in the revolt. It should focus on why you're so angry about the life you lead. In your opinion, is one reason more important than the others? If so, focus on this one a bit more.

   b Design a poster that tries to persuade fellow villagers to support the revolt.

   c Make a list of slogans that you might sing, chant, or write on banners that you might carry while marching to London.

Power to the people

In 1381, 14-year-old King Richard II decided he needed money for his war against France – all those weapons, armour and equipment were expensive! He asked his officials to make lists of the people living in each town and village, and then got his tax collectors to go round the country collecting money from anyone over the age of 15 to help pay for his costly war.

The new Poll Tax (a list is sometimes called a 'poll') was hated, especially by the poor, who said they couldn't afford to pay it.

Mission Objectives

- Discover what happened to the angry peasants when they took their revolt to London.
- Examine evidence and identify similarities and differences.

Chaos in the streets of London

The Peasants' Revolt started in May 1381 when peasants in Essex refused to pay the Poll Tax. This led to more attacks and the situation soon escalated! Read through the story below to find out what happened next.

1 Peasants began rebelling all over the south-east of England.

Who do these peasants think they are?

Fire! Fire! Fire!

2 Peasants burned important documents, books and papers.

He'll have no records at all!

Now the Lord won't know who to tax.

3 Some peasants broke into Maidstone prison and freed a priest called John Ball.

You're free!

Come and join us, We're off to London.

Ball had been put in prison for encouraging the poor to rebel against their lords.

4 In June, up to 60,000 peasants marched towards London. They chose a former soldier called Wat Tyler as their leader. The gatekeepers at London let the peasants into the city, as they didn't like the rich lords either.

What's the plan when we get there?

Tyler says he'll meet with the king and get him to make our lives better.

I want taxes reduced!

5 The angry mob ran riot. They burned down the houses of rich Londoners.

Let's go and attack the Tower of London!

6 Meanwhile, the king watched the rioting from the safety of the Tower of London. But…

I must go and meet them.

I suggest you meet them in a place where they cannot get near you.

But it's not safe, my lord!

7 The king decided to meet the peasants and spoke to them on a boat on the River Thames.

What do you want?

We want you to be our king… but we cannot stand how we are treated any longer.

8 Tyler told the king that peasants wanted higher wages and didn't want to be forced to work for their lords for free for a few days a week.

I agree to your demands and forgive you… but go home!

Can we trust him?

It is dangerous here, my Lord. Let's return to the Tower of London.

9 Meanwhile, a group of peasants broke into the Tower of London and murdered both the Archbishop of Canterbury and the king's treasurer.

The king's not back yet, but the man who looks after the king's money is here… so is the Archbishop of Canterbury.

Die, you traitor!

Arghh…

10 When the king realized that even the Tower of London wasn't safe, he knew he had to meet the rebels once more.

Tyler! The mob has murdered people. This must stop. Tell me what you want!

What happened next?

On 15 June 1381, the king once again met with Wat Tyler, who was joined by around 25,000 peasants. With the king were around 75 knights and nobles, including the Lord Mayor of London. Tyler asked the king to divide up all Church land amongst the peasants and make everyone, with the exception of the king, equal. The king agreed!

We are not *exactly* sure what happened next, as the only people who wrote about the event were on the king's side. However, the events of the next few minutes of the meeting were amazing. Read **Sources A** and **B** to see if you can work out what happened.

'At that moment the Mayor of London arrived with 12 knights, all well armed, and broke through to speak to the crowd. He said to Tyler, "Halt! Would you dare to speak like that in front of the king?" The king began to get angry and told the Mayor, "Set hands on him." Tyler said to the Mayor, "What have I said to annoy you?" "You lying, stinking crook," said the Mayor. "Would you speak like that in front of the king? By my life, you'll pay dearly for it." And the Mayor drew his sword and struck Tyler such a blow to the head that he fell down at the feet of his horse. The knights clustered around him so that he couldn't be seen by the rebels. Then a squire called John Standish drew out his sword and put it to Tyler's belly and so he died. Seeing their leader killed, the people began to murmur and said, "Let us go and kill them all." And they got themselves ready for battle.'

▲ **SOURCE A:** *This was written by Jean Froissant, a French knight, who wasn't at the revolt.*

'The commons were arrayed in battle formation in great numbers. Tyler dismounted, carrying his dagger. He called for some water and rinsed his mouth in a very rude disgusting fashion in front of the king. Tyler then made to strike the king's valet [bodyguard] with his dagger. The Mayor of London tried to arrest him, and because of this Wat stabbed the Mayor with his dagger in the stomach. But the Mayor, as it pleased God, was wearing armour, and drew his cutlass and gave Wat a deep cut on the neck, and then a great cut on the head.'

▲ **SOURCE B:** *A different account of the meeting in June 1381, written in the City Record Book.*

SOURCE C: *This picture is taken from an account of the murder of Wat Tyler and was painted 60 years after it happened. It is in two parts. On the left, King Richard II sees the murder and on the right he rides out to speak to the rebels.*

The aftermath

As you can imagine, the rebels were shocked by Wat Tyler's death and some looked ready to attack the king. Despite this, the king rode out to them, alone, and said, 'Sirs, what is the matter? You shall have no leader except me. I am your king. Be peaceful.' (See **Source C**.)

Almost immediately, the situation calmed down and shortly afterwards, the peasants began to go home.

But King Richard didn't keep any of the promises he'd made. His army hunted down many of the ringleaders of the revolt and killed them. John Ball, the priest, was cut into pieces in front of the king and his head was stuck on a spike on London Bridge. It was joined by the head of Wat Tyler! However, the hated Poll Tax was scrapped and taxes were never as high again.

Also, over the next 50 years the peasants ended up getting most of the things they asked for. Eventually, Parliament stopped trying to control peasants' wages and they were allowed to work for the best wages they could get.

Some peasants bought or rented land from a landowner. Having their own land meant they didn't have to rely on a lord to give them land – which meant they didn't have to work for him for free for a few days a week in return! Gradually, peasants became more independent and relied less on a lord to run all aspects of their lives – which is what the peasants who took part in the Peasants' Revolt really wanted!

Be a Top Historian

Top historians need to understand that it's very difficult to know *exactly* what happened at the Peasants' Revolt. Different people tell different stories depending on their attitudes and beliefs. Some details might be left out while others are exaggerated. This is why it's very important to try and find out about the person writing the account – who are they? What might they believe? Whose side might they be on?

Work

1 Match up the names on the left with the correct descriptions on the right.

• Wat Tyler	• 14-year-old king
• John Ball	• Killed Wat Tyler
• Richard II	• Leader of the Peasants' Revolt
• Mayor of London	• Priest who believed all men were equal and should not be forced to work for free

2 Read **Sources A** and **B**.
   a Find two ways in which the two sources are different.
   b Find two ways in which the two sources back each other up.
   c The two sources were written by people who supported the king. How might that affect what was written?
   d Why do you think no peasants wrote down what happened on 15 June 1381?

3 Look at **Source C**.
   a What does the picture show?
   b Does the source tell us anything about the character of Richard II?

4 **EITHER:** Imagine you were one of the peasants who marched to London with Wat Tyler. The revolt is over and you are back at home in your village… but the villagers who didn't go with you are keen to know what happened. Write down what you would tell them – and remember to make it accurate *and* exciting!

   OR: Finish off the cartoon strip on pages 118 and 119. You will notice that the final cartoon ends with King Richard II meeting with the peasants on 15 June 1381. But, as you know, such a lot happened at that meeting… and afterwards. Complete the cartoon strip by adding another two to five pictures to explain what happened next.

Assessing Your Learning 2

Was King John really such a bad king?

In History, a lot of what we know about people or events in the past comes from what people wrote down at the time. But historians (like us) have to be careful! We have to know about something called **interpretation**. Basically, this means that the person who wrote down what we're reading about someone (or something) gave their *opinion* at the same time. For example, if a monk didn't like a baron, he might write bad things about the baron. And two people can have very different views – or interpretations – of the same person. For example, if two people, supporting rival football teams, watched the two sides play each other, they would *interpret* the match differently. So, it is the job of the historian to:

- show **how** opinions (or interpretations) are different
- explain **why** opinions are different.

So what's this got to do with King John?

King John, who ruled between 1199 and 1216, is an ideal person to show how opinions of people at the time can influence our view of someone today. **Source A** demonstrates what lots of people think about King John today.

But where does this view come from?

Many of the bad things written about John were based on a book written in Victorian times (see **Source B**).

So where did the man who wrote Source B get his information from?

J.R. Green never met King John or knew anyone who did. He got his information from books written by monks who were alive at the time of John (see **Sources C** and **D**).

'John is generally looked upon as the worst king England ever had. He probably deserved the title. Although he was good looking and clever, he was a complete scoundrel and a selfish fool.'

▲ **SOURCE A:** *From a modern history book.*

'He was cruel. His punishments included the starvation of children and the crushing of old men under heavy weights. No women were safe near him and he scoffed at [mocked] priests. Hell itself is made worse by the presence of King John.'

▲ **SOURCE B:** *Written in 1874 by J.R. Green.*

'The servants brought a robber to King John. The robber had murdered a priest. John said, "He has killed an enemy of mine, let him go."

In 1209, Geoffrey, a priest, said it wasn't safe to work for King John and when John found out Geoffrey was imprisoned and starved. He died an agonizing death.'

▲ **SOURCE C:** *Written in the 1200s by Roger Wendover, a monk. Note that the 'Geoffrey' mentioned in this source did not die until nine years after King John!*

'John was a tyrant, a destroyer who crushed his own people… He hated his wife and she him. He gave orders that her lovers were to be killed on her bed.'

▲ **SOURCE D:** *Written by Matthew Paris, a monk, in the 1200s.*

Can we trust Sources C and D?

To decide how reliable the sources are, it is important to know that John quarrelled a lot with monks and taxed churches heavily. Matthew Paris, the monk who wrote **Source D**, was also the supporter of a group of barons who rebelled against King John.

Was anything else written about King John at the time?

Not a lot was written about John, but **Source E** is a picture of him created at the time and **Source F** is one of the orders he gave. Do these two sources surprise you?

Over to you

Now it's time to think about the sources and analyse *how* and *why* opinions (or interpretations) of King John might have changed over the centuries.

SOURCE E: *King John and his dogs.*

'The Jews living in your city are in your care. If anyone attempt to harm them, always protect and assist them.'

▲ **SOURCE F:** *John's orders to an English city.*

Work

1 Look at **Sources A** to **D**.
   a Find three opinions (or interpretations) about what sort of a man King John was.
   b Are there any facts in the sources, or just opinions?

2 Look at **Sources B**, **C**, and **D**.
   a Is there anything in **Source B** that makes you think that the writer might have read **Sources C** and **D**?
   b Can **Sources C** and **D** be totally trusted? Give reasons for your answer.

3 Look at **Sources E** and **F**.
   a What impression of King John do these sources give you?
   b If all you knew about King John was what was shown in **Sources E** and **F**, would **Sources A** to **D** surprise you? Give reasons for your answer.

4 a Read **Source A** again. Why do you think King John is often portrayed as a bad, evil king?
   b Is it possible to prove what King John was *really* like?

Assessing your work

In a **good** set of answers, you would…	• select and combine some information from different sources • structure your work well • show that you understand that people and events of the past can be interpreted in different ways.
In a **better** set of answers, you would…	• begin to **evaluate** different sources and use the ones that are **best suited** to the task • select and combine information from different sources • structure your work well • **suggest reasons** for some different interpretations of the past.
In the **best** set of answers, you would…	• evaluate sources well • select, organize and use different sources • structure your work well • explain **how and why** different interpretations of the past exist.

Hungry for More?

King John has been famously interpreted in different ways. Choose another historical figure and research different ways in which they have been interpreted. Oliver Cromwell, Emmeline Pankhurst and Richard III are good examples.

7.1A We're all going to die!

In the spring of 1348 the people of Britain were gripped by fear. A killer disease was spreading across the country and killing thousands and thousands of people. Whole villages were being wiped out and no one seemed able to stop it. The disease was known as 'Black Death' and it would go on to kill around one out of every three people!

Mission Objectives

- Define the main symptoms of Black Death.
- Discover what people thought caused the disease at the time and how they tried to protect against it.

Read the following accounts of the impact the disease had on people. Victims of Black Death really did suffer from the symptoms described by the villagers pictured here. Also, the causes of the disease were all genuinely believed by people at the time. As you will discover, it is no wonder people were so scared…

> It's 12 August 1348 and I am so worried. Father Peter has visited most of the houses in the village and says that lots of people have been unable to work today. He says many people are hot and sweaty, like they have a fever, and that their muscles and bones ache. We are to pray that it is not the terrible disease that everyone is talking about. My friend Eleanor tells me that her mother has the fever.

1

- Emma Langdale, a baker's wife
- 28 years old
- Three children

2

- Eleanor Carter, who works for the local landowner
- 26 years old
- Married, two children

> Seven more families in the village are ill today. My mother, who had a fever yesterday, has found boils under her armpits and in her groin. I've been told that some people have found boils as big as apples. Father Peter has been mixing up some soothing ointments to smear over the boils, so perhaps that will help.

3

- Father Peter, local priest

> More and more people are becoming ill. And it attacks anyone — rich and poor, good and bad. Just yesterday, I was called to Emma Langdale's bakery because her little boy has a fever. Why him, O Lord? What harm has he ever done? And Eleanor Carter's mother is now covered in a red and black rash. She says she tried to stick a needle into one of the boils last night but it wouldn't burst. Nothing seems to work.

④

- Sir James Bickley, local landowner
- Owns lots of land that the villagers work on
- Married, three children

It's 15 August today and it's like the whole village is ill. It seemed to start three or four days ago after the weekly market in the centre of the village. I wonder if anyone from other villages who came to buy and sell here that day was poorly. The Langdale family, who run the bakery, have been badly hit. They're all poorly, but their little boy is particularly ill. Boils have appeared on his body and his breath smells foul. He has terrible diarrhoea too. What sins have we committed? Have we danced or drunk too much? God is punishing us all!

⑤

- Adam Smith, village blacksmith
- 48 years old
- Husband, father and grandfather

People are dying! Twelve died during the night and three more already today, including Eleanor Carter's mother. Before she died, she was screaming for water. Eleanor gave her some, but her throat was so swollen that she couldn't swallow. Perhaps God punished her for drinking ale on Sundays. Eleanor said that the boils under her arms burst as she died and smelly black pus dripped onto the deathbed. All the Carters are ill now and I fear for their lives.

⑥

- John Edwards , works for Sir James
- Married, four children

It's been a week since Ellie Carter's mother became ill... and now she's dead! Someone told me that Ellie herself has huge boils as big as onions under her arms too. The Langdales are suffering too. The young boy has been covered in a rash for a few days now and his boils are getting bigger. Perhaps he's close to death. I know Emma Langdale and her older daughter are in bed today with a fever and even Father Peter is ill. I'm worried about my youngest son who was up all night sweating and sneezing.

We have decided to dig a large pit just outside the village in which to bury all the dead. But will it be big enough? Will anyone survive? Perhaps we're all going to die!

Work

1 Write a sentence to explain the word 'symptom' using a modern-day example of a common symptom of an illness in your answer.

2 a From what you have read, identify at least five symptoms of Black Death. Try to put them in the order in which a victim would get them.

   b Can you think of any reasons why the disease was called 'Black Death'?

3 a In what ways did people try to treat the disease?

   b List any reasons why people thought someone might catch Black Death.

7.1B We're all going to die!

So what exactly was Black Death?

The Black Death was a plague, which is a disease that spreads quickly. In fact, to be more accurate, experts who have studied the illness think that Black Death was **two** different plagues that struck at the same time.

Bubonic plague

- This is a germ which lived in the blood of black rats and in the fleas on their bodies.
- The fleas would hop off the rats onto humans and bite them… passing on the disease.
- Victims would get a fever and large boils (called 'buboes') in their armpits, groin and behind their ears. Then the victim would develop a rash of red and black spots.
- The illness lasted about a week. Seven out of ten people would die.

Ow! Something bit me!

Pneumonic plague

- Also a deadly germ, it travelled in the air. It was caught by breathing infected air.
- It attacked the lungs, causing victims to cough up blood and spread deadly germs as they sneezed.
- The victims' breath would smell as their lungs rotted inside them.
- Victims would die within a week.

aaaachOO!!

A deadly combination

Bubonic and pneumonic plague combined to make Black Death. It was possible to get one plague without the other but pneumonic plague was so deadly that if you caught it you'd probably die anyway. About 30 per cent of people who caught only bubonic plague survived. But sadly, millions all over the world caught both plagues at the same time and stood no chance!

What did people think caused Black Death?

Doctors didn't know that germs caused disease so looked for other reasons to explain why something so terrible was happening. **Sources A** to **E** show the different ways in which people at the time tried to explain the cause of Black Death.

'The plague was a punishment from God.'

▲ **SOURCE A:** *By a medieval Italian writer.*

'In many German cities, Jews were thought to have caused the deaths by poisoning the water supply. Many Jewish men, women and children were burned to death for this.'

▲ **SOURCE B:** *From a book written in 1349.*

'You should avoid overeating and avoid having a bath. These open up the pores of the skin through which the poisonous air can enter.'

▲ **SOURCE C:** *A French writer, 1365.*

'The long term cause is the position of the planets. It is also caused by evil smells which mix with the air and spread on the wind. When you breathe in the corrupted air you catch the plague.'

▲ **SOURCE D:** *Based on a report written by doctors at Paris University in 1348.*

'The disease was spread by contagion. If a healthy man visited a plague victim, he usually died himself.'

▲ **SOURCE E:** *Written by Jean de Venette around 1348.*

How did people try to 'cure' the plague?

There were all sorts of 'cures' suggested. It's easy to laugh at some of them, but try to appreciate that people were scared – not stupid – and were prepared to try anything.

> My doctor told me to drink vinegar and mercury.

> I've been told that shaving a chicken's bottom and strapping it to the boils will do the trick.

> Why not kill all the cats and dogs?

> If you pop them, they go away apparently.

> Just kill a toad, dry it in the sun, hold it on your boils and watch the poison get sucked out.

SOURCE F: *In Europe, large groups of people called **flagellants** went around whipping themselves, hoping that God would take pity on them and stop the plague!*

Wise Up Words

bubonic   pneumonic

Work

1 Copy and complete the following table.

	Bubonic plague	Pneumonic plague
How was it caught?		
What were the symptoms?		
How long did it take to die?		

2 Look at **Sources A** to **E**.

a Make a list of all the different explanations that people in the Middle Ages gave for the cause of Black Death.

b Why do you think there were so many different explanations of the cause of Black Death?

c Which explanation comes closest to the real cause of plague?

3 Design a Black Death information leaflet for 1348. Remember that nobody knew what we do about the causes of the plague, so don't mention fleas, germs or rats. Your leaflet should:

- warn people about the causes – add pictures to make the message stronger
- advise people about the cures available
- be eye-catching and informative.

Remember that few people at the time could read. How does this affect the sort of leaflet you will create?

7.2 How deadly was Black Death?

Black Death was perhaps the worst disaster of the Middle Ages. Worldwide, it killed around 75 million people. In Europe, about 25 million people died (around half of the population). In Britain, at least two million people died in just one year... which was about one third of all people in the country. But where did Black Death come from? And how did it spread?

The map on this page shows how the plague spread into Europe. Historians think that the disease probably started in Asia (possibly China) and was carried by infected rats and people on ships that were transporting goods like spices and cloth into Europe.

Try to match up the medieval descriptions of the spread of Black Death (**Sources B** to **E**) with the correct number on the map.

FACT!

As you know, Black Death was actually two plagues (bubonic and pneumonic) attacking at the same time. But did you know that both plagues still exist today? Thankfully, both can be treated if medical attention is sought quickly!

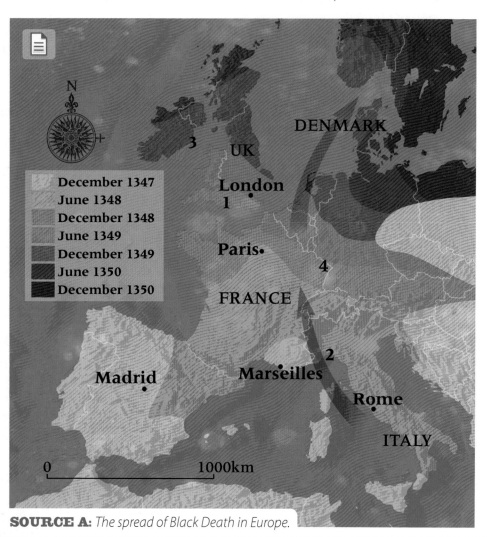

Map legend:
- December 1347
- June 1348
- December 1348
- June 1349
- December 1349
- June 1350
- December 1350

0 — 1000km

SOURCE A: *The spread of Black Death in Europe.*

'In January of the year 1348, three galleys [ships] put in at Genoa, Italy. They had come from the East and were horribly infected with the Plague. No one would go near the ships, even though they had a valuable cargo of spices and other goods.'

▲ **SOURCE B:** *Medieval description of Black Death.*

'Jews were burned in Strasbourg, Germany. It was believed that they had caused the plague by poisoning drinking water.'

▲ **SOURCE C:** *From the chronicle of Neuberg monastery, written at the time of Black Death.*

'In this year at Melcombe [now Weymouth] Dorset, a little before the feast of St John the Baptist [24 June], two ships came into the harbour. One of the sailors had brought him, from Gascony in France, the disease, and through him the people of Melcombe were the first in England to be infected.'

▲ **SOURCE D:** *From the* Grey Friars Chronicle, *written by monks in 1348.*

'The cities of Dublin and Drogheda were almost entirely destroyed and wasted of men... There was scarcely a house in which only one died and commonly man, wife and children went one way, crossing to death.'

▲ **SOURCE E:** *Friar John Clyn, 1348.*

Be a Top Historian

Top historians can use information written by people at the time to analyse the past. Here we're using sources to show where the plague spread to. Some of the sources also give us clues about the impact of Black Death and how people at the time blamed Jewish people for starting the plague.

Black Death disaster

Black Death affected all sorts of people – rich and poor, adults and children. No one was safe. Sometimes whole villages were wiped out. In places, fields and streets were littered with bodies and houses stood silent and empty.

Within a year, Britain's population plunged from around five million to three million. And it kept falling as small outbreaks of plague hit Britain in 1361, 1368, 1371, 1373 and 1390. By 1450, there were barely two-and-a-half million people left.

Find out about one of the recent outbreaks of pneumonic or bubonic plague. Where was it? How many were infected? How were people treated?

Hungry for More?

Work

1 Match up **Sources B**, **C**, **D**, and **E** with the correct place number on the map (**Source A**). An atlas might help you with this.

2 **a** How do historians think the plague arrived in Europe?
 b How do you think the plague got into England? (Does one of the sources help you with your answer here? If so, say which one.)

3 Using the map and sources on these pages, write an essay that explains how Black Death spread. Remember to plan your work and structure your writing into paragraphs.

Who healed the sick in the Middle Ages?

It is 1350 and you feel ill. If you are poor you might ask people in your village if they know of any treatments. You will probably get a variety of answers telling you to try all sorts of strange herbs, plants and potions. Some might even make you feel a bit better. But if your neighbours don't help, you might try praying a bit harder or plan a pilgrimage to a holy place and hope that God might cure you. As a last resort, you might take what money you have and travel to the nearest town to see the doctor.

However, he won't have modern drugs like antibiotics or any antiseptic to prevent infection. He doesn't know that germs and viruses make us ill either. In fact, he doesn't know much about the real causes of illness at all. So what will he do to make you feel better?

Mission Objectives

- Investigate the theories behind different treatments in the Middle Ages.
- Evaluate ways in which doctors diagnosed illness in the Middle Ages.

Trying to work out what's wrong

He would probably examine your blood too, look at your tongue and take your pulse… although he wouldn't really know what he was looking for!

To find out what was wrong with you, the doctor would probably ask you to wee in a clear glass bottle.
He would then examine it three times – once when it's fresh, again when it has been cooling for about an hour, and finally when it has gone completely cold. He might even taste it to see if it was sweet or sour, bitter or salty.

He might even ask you to poo on a tray so he could have a good look through it… but, again, he wouldn't really know what he was looking for!

Your doctor would then go off to look at his charts and flick through his books. The colour of your urine would be matched against the shades on a special diagram – they did this because they thought that every shade had a different meaning.

FACT!

Good doctors were in short supply and could be expensive. This left things open for 'quacks', people who sold all sorts of potions that were supposed to cure everything. These potions were sold at fairs and by the side of roads… and usually contained nothing at all to help you to get better!

Bad blood

Doctors often thought that your own blood was the cause of illness. This was based on an old Greek idea that a person's **humours** (main liquids in the body, of which blood was one) could be out of balance and cause illness. Many doctors thought that the answer was to make the patient bleed, so that their 'bad' blood would disappear and their body would be in balance again. This was called **bloodletting** and special tools and bowls were used to cut open a vein and bleed a patient (see **Source A**). Sometimes **leeches** were used to suck the blood out too. If you were selected for a bleeding session you would pray your doctor was skilled enough to know when to stop before you lost too much blood!

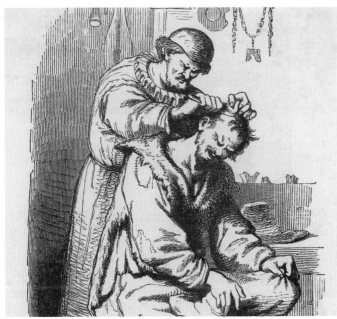

SOURCE A: *If your doctor recommended a bloodletting session, you might get the job done by a* **barber-surgeon***. He was usually a bit cheaper than a doctor and you could have your hair cut at the same time (sharp knives, you see!). His shop would be easy to spot because it had a red and white pole outside (red for blood, white for bandages). Some barbers still have poles like these outside their shops today.*

> *'If you would strength and fitness keep, shun care and anger while you sleep. All heavy food and wine give up, and noon day slumber too must stop. Walk awhile each day you should, for this will only do you good. These rules obey and you will find, long life is yours and peaceful mind.'*

▲ **SOURCE D:** *A medieval poem which proves that there were some ideas about health and fitness long ago that still stand today.*

Wise Up Words

apothecary   barber-surgeon   bloodletting
humours   leech   purging   trepanning

> *'A doctor must know how to read so that he can understand medical books. He must know how to write and speak well so that he can explain the diseases he is treating. He must have a good mind to investigate and cure the causes of disease. Arithmetic is also important, so that he can be a great help to the sick… Lastly, he must know astronomy so that he can study the stars and the seasons, because our bodies change with the planets and stars.'*

▲ **SOURCE B:** *An early medieval writer.*

> *'Doctors possess three special qualifications and these are: to be able to lie without being caught out; to pretend to be honest; and to cause death without feeling guilty.'*

▲ **SOURCE C:** *Written in 1380.*

Work

1   Look at **Source A**. In your own words, describe what's going on in the picture.

2   Read **Source B**.
   a   Make a list of the skills required by a doctor in the Middle Ages. Put them in order of how useful they would be when trying to cure people.
   b   Do you think a modern doctor needs the same skills? Explain your answer.

3   Read **Source C**.
   a   What is this person's opinion of doctors in 1380?
   b   Can you think of any reasons why the person might have thought this?

4   Read **Source D**.
   a   What four things does the writer advise people to do to keep fit and healthy?
   b   Do *you* think you could do anything else to keep fit and healthy?

Terrifying treatments

Some doctors might have even tried treatments which sound terrifying today. They might have tried **purging** you, which meant giving you something to eat to make you vomit or go to the toilet a lot. The idea was to get the 'badness' out of your body (see **Source A**). And if you had a headache, the doctor might try **trepanning** – he would drill a hole (yes, drill a hole!) in your head to let out the evil spirits that were making your head sore (see **Source D**). However, he would make sure he consulted his Zodiac chart to check he was operating on you when it was safe to do so (see **Source C**). **Source B** gives some more strange treatments from the Middle Ages.

SOURCE A: *A doctor 'purging' a patient.*

◀ **SOURCE B:** *Medieval treatments published in a book during the Middle Ages.*

For an ache that is found in the teeth, take a whole corn of pepper and chew on them.

For swollen eyes, take a live crab, poke out its eyes and put it back in the water. Stick the eyes onto your neck and you will be well.

For wheezing and shortness of breath, kill a fox and take out its liver and lungs. Chop them up and mix it with wine. Then drink the mixture out of a church bell.

If you are bitten by a snake, smear ear wax on the bite, then ask the priest to say a prayer for you. If you accidentally drink an insect in the water, find a sheep, cut into it and drink the blood while it's still hot. If you take good long gulps, all will be well.

For warts, hold a live toad next to the skin and soon your skin will soften and the warts will disappear.

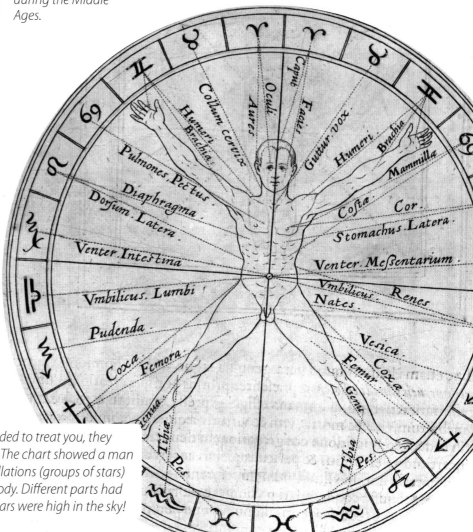

SOURCE C: *A zodiac chart. If doctors needed to treat you, they would use a zodiac chart to find a safe date. The chart showed a man surrounded by figures to show which constellations (groups of stars) were thought to 'rule' different parts of the body. Different parts had to be left alone during the time when their stars were high in the sky!*

Herbal treatments

As you may have worked out, visiting a doctor could be a risky business (see **Source E**), and many of the treatments had no real chance of working. But doctors weren't the only people treating the sick. **Apothecaries** were specialist medicine-makers who experimented with plants and herbs – like poppy, willow leaves and garlic – to treat people. And today we know that they must have had real success. Modern scientists recently analysed a medieval apothecary book and concluded that over half of the herbal remedies prescribed to ease pain and help fight infection would have actually worked. Poppies and willow leaves, for example, contain a natural form of painkiller, whilst garlic is known to kill bacteria.

SOURCE D: A medieval 'cure' for a headache.

Poppy

Willow leaves

Garlic

'An Arab doctor was asked to treat a knight with a cut on his leg and a woman with lung disease. He cleaned the knight's leg and put a fresh dressing on it and changed the woman's diet to make her feel better.

A European doctor appeared and laughed at the Arab doctor's ideas. He told the knight that it would be better for him to live with one leg than not to live at all and ordered that the wounded leg should be removed. The knight died with one swing of the axe.

The European doctor then cut open the woman's skull and removed her brain. He rubbed the brain with salt, claiming that this would wash away the devil inside her. The woman, of course, died instantly.'

▲ **SOURCE E:** European and Arab treatments are described in a story written by a Muslim.

FACT!

Surgeons were often viewed as being no better than butchers. They didn't need to go to university but did need to pass a test to get their licence. They pulled teeth, lanced boils, treated burns, set broken bones, and let blood. Military surgeons were experts at removing arrowheads and repairing cuts.

Work

1 Make a list of at least five different treatments used by medieval doctors to try and cure people. For each treatment, see if you can explain why a doctor might have believed the treatment would work.

2 a What was the difference between a barber-surgeon and an apothecary?
  b Which one would you rather visit if you were sick?

3 Look at **Sources A** and **D**.
  a What is happening in each picture?
  b Why is the doctor trying to cure his patients using these methods?

4 Read **Source E**.
  a Who appears to have the best understanding of medicine – the European doctor or the Arab doctor? Explain your answer.
  b European doctors' understanding of medicine improved greatly after many years of war against the Arabs. Why do you think this might have happened?

5 **The Big Write!**

In pairs write a short script for a role-play activity about a sick person's visit to the doctor in the Middle Ages. One person should act out the role of the patient, the other the role of the doctor. Look back at this section for some gruesome ideas!

Was it dangerous to be the king?

Would you like to have been a King of England during the Middle Ages? Surely it was one of the best jobs in the world – a luxurious lifestyle with the best clothes, the finest homes and the tastiest food. You would have all the brightest, best and most hard-working people in the land to attend to your every need. But could a king's great status, wealth and power buy him a long and happy life? Indeed, just how dangerous was it to be King of England in the Middle Ages?

Mission Objectives

- Develop an opinion – do you think England's medieval kings were a particularly healthy bunch?

King Harold II of England (1066)

Killed fighting at the Battle of Hastings.

William I (1066–1087)

Killed in France when his bladder burst in a riding accident. Died in agony.

William II (1087–1100)

Son of William I. Shot and killed by an arrow in a hunting accident.

Some historians think he may have been murdered, though!

Henry I (1100–1135)

Younger brother of William II. Spent a lot of time fighting.

Died of eating too much.

Stephen (1135–1154)

Grandson of William I, nephew of Henry I. Spent most of his time fighting for the throne against his cousin Matilda (who ruled briefly in 1141).

Died of a stomach infection and internal bleeding.

Edward IV (1461–1470 and 1471–1483)

Great-great-grandson of Edward III. Fought the Wars of the Roses. Caught a fever after going to bed because he'd eaten too much.

Henry VI (1422–1461 and 1470–1471)

Son of Henry V. Fought the Wars of the Roses. Went mad, lost his throne twice and was murdered in the Tower of London.

Henry V (1413–1422)

Son of Henry IV. Died of dysentery while fighting in France.

Henry IV (1399–1413)

Cousin of Richard II. Henry had lots of illnesses during the last few years of his life, possibly including leprosy (a disfiguring skin disease).

Edward V (1483)

Son of Edward IV. Disappeared aged 12, possibly suffocated or died of a mystery illness.

Richard III (1483–1485)

Brother of Edward IV, uncle of Edward V. Killed while fighting at the Battle of Bosworth Field, near Leicester.

Henry VII (1485–1509)

Great-great-great-grandson of Edward III. Ended the Wars of the Roses by marrying Elizabeth of York, a member of the opposing family. Died of tuberculosis and replaced by his son, Henry VIII.

Historians give names to the different groups or families who ruled England between 1066 and 1509. This also makes it easier to remember the stories about them.

KEY

- Harold – Anglo-Saxon
- Norman, because they first lived in Normandy, France
- Plantagenet – family name
- Lancaster – family name
- York – family name
- Tudor – family name

Note: The dates in the diagram are the dates of his reign, not his life.

Work

1 a Make notes of how many kings were killed by the following:
- battle
- accident
- eating too much
- murder
- old age
- illness

b Draw a bar chart to show your findings.

c What was the biggest cause of death? Why do you think this?

2 Which cause of death surprises you the most? Explain your answer.

3 Write a paragraph to explain whether or not you think that being a medieval King of England was a dangerous job, giving your reasons.

Henry II (1154–1189)
Son of Matilda, grandson of Henry I. Spent years fighting with his wife and sons.
Died from a bleeding stomach ulcer while fighting in France.

Richard I (The Lionheart) (1189–1199)
Son of Henry II. Shot in the neck by a crossbow bolt while fighting in France. The wound became infected when doctors tried to treat him. Died as a result of the infection.

John (1199–1216)
Brother of Richard I. Spent a lot of his time fighting wars in France and arguing with his barons.
Died from dysentery, a nasty form of diarrhoea.

Henry III (1216–1272)
Son of King John. Thrown in prison by rebel barons in 1264, but regained his throne.
Died of old age, possibly a stroke.

Edward I (Hammer of the Scots) (1272–1307)
Son of Henry III. Died of dysentery on his way to fight the Scots.

Edward II (1307–1327)
Son of Edward I. Lost all the land in Scotland that his father had won. Hated by his wife Isabella, who wanted their son (also named Edward) to be king instead. She eventually killed him by ordering two men to either suffocate him… or stick a red-hot piece of iron up his bottom!

Edward III (1327–1377)
Son of Edward II. Ruled during the Black Death. Died aged 64 of a stroke.

Richard II (1377–1399)
Grandson of Edward III. Had no children. His cousin Henry (also the grandson of Edward III) fought Richard II for the throne. Henry eventually beat Richard and became Henry IV. Richard was put in prison at Pontefract Castle and starved to death.

DO NOT FEED

Hungry for More?

The diagram looks at 20 kings and mentions one queen (remember Matilda?). Five of the rulers were under 15 years of age when they became king. But who were they? Try to find out the names and ages of the five youngest kings – one was only nine months old. He sat on his mother's knee and cried when he was crowned! Another king's head was so small that they had to use a bracelet as a crown!

Assessing Your Learning 3

What were the consequences of Black Death?

As historians, you will know that events (like wars or rebellions) usually have lots of different **causes**. You should also know that there are often lots of different results of an event when it takes place. These results are sometimes called 'effects' or 'consequences'. This assessment is going to look at the **consequences** of Black Death, the killer disease that hit Britain in the fourteenth century. Look at the sources carefully and answer the questions that follow.

'Sheep and oxen wandered free through the fields and among the crops, and there was nobody to drive them off... When harvest time came, higher wages were not enough to get people to gather in the crops which rotted in the fields.'

▲ **SOURCE A:** *From* Knighton's Chronicle *1337–1396 by Henry Knighton.*

'At the deserted village of Wyville in Lincolnshire the land is worth little because it is poor and stony. It is not being used because there are no people left to farm it after the plague.'

▲ **SOURCE B:** *From the records of Eynsham Abbey, around 1385.*

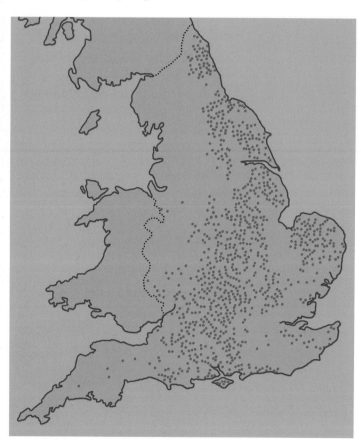

SOURCE C: *This map shows the number of deserted medieval villages after the plague had killed their inhabitants.*

'The King sent an order to all the counties that labourers should not be paid more than before the plague. But the labourers were so proud and stubborn that they would not listen to the king's command. If anyone wanted to employ then he had to pay them what they wanted or lose his fruit and crops... Then the king ordered many labourers to be arrested and put in prison.'

▲ **SOURCE D:** *From* Knighton's Chronicle *1337–1396 by Henry Knighton.*

'It is sad but the whole world was changed for the worse. People were meaner and more greedy than before, even though they had more things. They were jealous of each other and there was an increase in the number of fights, arguments and law cases.'

▲ **SOURCE E:** *Written by Jean de Venette around 1348.*

Year	Wages for farm work
1346	5 pence
1349	5 pence
1353	10 pence

SOURCE F: *A table showing the increase in wages for farm workers after Black Death had passed. The workers who survived realized that there were lots of jobs for them because there were fewer people around to do the work. So workers began to ask for more money to do the same jobs. The lords had to pay them the extra money or risk all their crops rotting in the fields!*

'As soon as masters accuse their workers of bad work or try to pay them less they leave and quickly find jobs in new places at higher wages. Masters dare not upset their workers and have to give them whatever they ask for.'

▲ **SOURCE G:** *The introduction to a law from 1376.*

Over to you

Now it's time to analyse the sources and think about what they tell us about the effects of Black Death.

Work

1 Firstly, copy out and complete the table below, which gives some of the effects of Black Death. Read each source again and tick the effects that it mentions.

Effect / Source	Some villages were deserted	There was a shortage of workers	People wanted higher wages	People became mean and greedy
A				
B				
C				

2 The king has asked you to write him a brief report (no more than 200 words) on the consequences of Black Death. Use the sources on these pages to help you.

Assessing your work

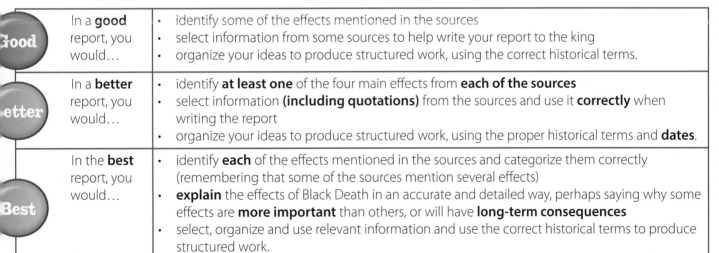

Good	In a **good** report, you would…	• identify some of the effects mentioned in the sources • select information from some sources to help write your report to the king • organize your ideas to produce structured work, using the correct historical terms.
Better	In a **better** report, you would…	• identify **at least one** of the four main effects from **each of the sources** • select information **(including quotations)** from the sources and use it **correctly** when writing the report • organize your ideas to produce structured work, using the proper historical terms and **dates**.
Best	In the **best** report, you would…	• identify **each** of the effects mentioned in the sources and categorize them correctly (remembering that some of the sources mention several effects) • **explain** the effects of Black Death in an accurate and detailed way, perhaps saying why some effects are **more important** than others, or will have **long-term consequences** • select, organize and use relevant information and use the correct historical terms to produce structured work.

Plague has hit Britain many times since the outbreak in the 1300s. Most famously, plague swept through London and other parts of Britain in 1665. Find out about another outbreak of plague. When was it? Where were outbreaks recorded? How many died?

Hungry for More?

Keeping law and order

The topic of crime and punishment is big news in today's world. The latest crime figures and the big murder trials are often on our television screens, the radio, and in our newspapers. Special TV programmes are dedicated to catching criminals or showing us how the criminal justice system works. We know that the police investigate crime and try to catch lawbreakers. Then the courts decide if a person is guilty or not and, if they are found guilty, decide on a punishment. This could be a fine or even prison.

But what was it like in the Middle Ages? How were criminals caught? And how were people punished?

Mission Objectives

- Recall how towns and villages tried to keep law and order in the Middle Ages.
- Compare medieval types of punishment with modern methods.

Keeping the peace

There were no policemen in the Middle Ages. If towns and villages wanted to keep law and order they had to do it themselves. If you ever saw someone committing a crime you had to raise the **hue and cry**. This meant that you had to shout loudly and people would come to help you track down or catch the criminal.

In some areas, all men and women over the age of twelve were put into groups of ten. These **tithings**, as they were known, were responsible for each other's behaviour. If a member of the tithing broke the law the others had to take him or her to court and pay their fines.

Some places set up a **watch** – a group of people who patrolled the streets each night – and a **constable** was chosen to coordinate them. But these weren't particularly popular jobs. People didn't get paid for a start… and you lost a lot of sleep whilst walking around the streets all night. As a result, constables and watchmen didn't always do their jobs properly – if they did, they might be chosen again.

Because there was no police force, criminals must have got away with very serious crimes as they were rarely caught. So sometimes even the king himself got involved in investigations. In 1129, for example, King Henry I fined four whole villages for not finding a murderer quickly enough.

'The township of Stansfield did not raise the hue and cry on the thieves that burgled the house of Amery of Hertelay, nor ever found or prosecuted them. They are to be fined 40 shillings.'

▲ **SOURCE A:** *From Wakefield Manor court records, October 1315.*

FACT!

Prison wasn't really a punishment in the Middle Ages because there weren't any prisons as we know them today. Some towns had a cell where captured criminals were kept until they were punished, but big prisons with hundreds of inmates didn't exist.

Punishment fits the crime

When a criminal was caught, they would usually be taken to the local lord's manor house. The lord would then decide on a punishment, which would usually be a fine. Sometimes, the lord would try to make the punishment fit the crime. So a person who sold bad wine might be forced to drink some while the rest was poured over their head. A baker who sold stale bread might be dragged through the streets with mouldy bread tied around their neck while people threw rotten food at him. Sometimes thieves had fingers cut off and people who told lies about their neighbours had their tongues cut out (see **Sources B** and **C**.)

While criminals could sit down in the **stocks**, prisoners had to stand up in the **pillory**. Sometimes a prisoner's ears were nailed to the wood or a large stone was hung around their neck; naughty children might be taken to a finger pillory, which trapped just the fingertips!

Wise Up Words

constable   hue and cry   pillory
stocks   tithing   watch

Nicholas Hopwood for hitting Magota, daughter of Henry – fined 2d.

Margaret Webb for breach of peace – fined 2d.

Amos Walter for theft of his lord's pigs. Also carrying a bow and arrow in his lord's wood – two fingers on right hand struck off; fined 2d for bow and arrow.

▲ **SOURCE B:** *The records of Rochdale Court, from November 1335, describe crimes and the related punishments. 'd' was a medieval way of writing 'p' for 'pence'. Two pence was a lot of money in the Middle Ages!*

SOURCE C: *Medieval punishments were often carried out in the middle of town to make other people think twice about commiting crimes themselves.*

Two drunks in the pillory

A man who sold bad bread

A man found guilty of assault

Work

1   Match each word or phrase from **List A** with the correct definition from **List B**.

List A	List B
Tithing	A loud noise to make people chase a criminal
Hue and cry	A group of ten people who are responsible for each othe
Stocks	An official who looked after law and order
Constable	A group who watched over a town
Watch	A wooden frame used to hold prisoners

2   What is meant by the phrase 'the punishment fitted the crime'? Give an example to go you're your answer

3   Explain the difference between the stocks and the pillory. Which one do you think a criminal would like least?

4   Look at **Source B**.
   a   What crimes has Amos Walter committed?
   b   Why do you think Amos was punished in this way?

Trial and punishment

In medieval times, most minor crimes were dealt with by the local lord. So, for example, a villager who let his pigs wander into another person's crops might be fined. But sometimes crimes were so serious that they were dealt with by one of the king's special courts – crimes such as murder, violent assault or major theft. These courts were known as Shire Courts or Royal Courts.

Serious stuff

A judge, appointed by the king, would travel to each county (perhaps twice a year) to deal with serious crimes. Working with advisors, the judge would look through the evidence, listen to witnesses, and come to a decision. If a judge thought a person was guilty, he could punish them any way he chose… and some of the punishments were brutal! **Source A** shows you the type of punishment a guilty person could expect for serious crimes.

Serious assault, forgery, repeated stealing

whipping   fingers, hands, ears cut off

Murder, very serious assault, stealing anything worth a lot of money

Men usually hanged (richer people often had their heads cut off)

Women usually burned

Treason (a crime against the king or country)

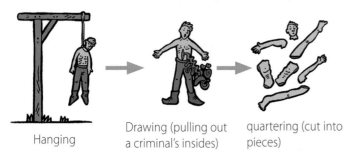

Hanging   Drawing (pulling out a criminal's insides)   quartering (cut into pieces)

SOURCE A: *Serious crimes were dealt with brutally.*

Trial by ordeal

Sometimes judges couldn't make up their minds about whether a person was guilty or not, so they would order a **trial by ordeal** as a way of letting God decide someone's guilt. Trial by ordeal, the judge felt, was a good way for God to help the innocent and punish the guilty. The most common trials by ordeal were fire, water and combat.

> **Ordeal by fire**
>
> **Step 1** The accused carries a red-hot iron bar for three steps, or takes a stone from the bottom of a pot of boiling water.
>
> **Step 2** The prisoner's hand is bandaged, and he returns to court three days later.
>
> **Verdict** If the wound has healed, God must think the prisoner is worth helping because he is innocent. If the wound is infected, God must think the prisoner is not worth helping and so he must be guilty. He must be punished by being put to death.

Ordeal by water

Step 1 The accused is tied up.

Step 2 He is thrown into a lake or river.

Verdict Water is pure, just like God. If the prisoner floats, the water doesn't want him, nor does God. If God has rejected him, he must be guilty, and must be put to death. If the prisoner sinks and drowns, God must want him in heaven. He must be innocent.

Trial by jury

Thankfully, trial by ordeal didn't last long. It was used less and less in the thirteenth century, when Church leaders objected to it. Instead they were gradually replaced by a system still used today – trial by **jury**. The jury was a group of 12 local men who had the job of saying whether the person was telling the truth or not. The judge then decided if the person was guilty. In later years, the jury would decide on a guilty or innocent verdict – something that still survives in today's crown courts.

Wise Up Words

jury   trial by ordeal

Ordeal by combat

This was a trial for rich people. The accuser would fight the accused. It was possible to get someone called a champion to fight for you. Some people did this for a living, earning huge amounts of money fighting on behalf of different lords.

Step 1 Both sides should select their weapons. These would be made from wood and bone.

Step 2 The accuser and the accused (or their champions) must fight for as long as possible, starting at sunrise.

Verdict People believed God would give the person telling the truth extra strength. The first person to surrender was thought to be guilty and therefore must be punished by being put to death.

FACT!

As you can see, God featured heavily in the criminal justice system. In fact, if you could read a verse from the Bible you were allowed to go on trial in a church court (usually reserved for naughty priests) and these often ordered lighter punishments than other courts

Work

1 Write down what sort of punishments these people might have received:
   a A woman who made fake coins
   b A rich male murderer
   c Someone who tried to kill the king
   d A man who kept stealing vegetables from his neighbour
   e A poor female murderer

2 a Why do you think many people in the Middle Ages believed that ordeals were a good way to find out if someone was guilty or not?
   b Do **you** think ordeals were a good way of finding out whether someone was guilty or not?

c Why do you think punishments at the time were so tough?
d What was 'trial by jury'? Do you think this was fairer than 'trial by ordeal'? Explain your view.

3 Imagine you work for one of the king's judges and you are about to visit a town for a series of trials.

EITHER: write a short speech

OR: design an information leaflet

explaining how the judge will try to find out whether a person is guilty or not.

Do you know anyone who has argued with their neighbours? Do you know why they quarrelled? Was it about house or garden boundaries? Or perhaps they just didn't get on with each other? The country of England has two next-door neighbours with whom it shares a border – Wales and Scotland – and Ireland is not very far away by sea, either. Not surprisingly, they haven't always got on with each other. In fact, in the Middle Ages, English kings tried to take over and control their neighbours. But why? How did they try to do it? And how successful were they?

Mission Objectives

- Identify how and why England tried to conquer Wales.
- Judge how successful these attempts were.

England versus Wales

In 1066, William the Conqueror won the Battle of Hastings and became King of England. At this time, Wales was a completely separate country from England. It had its own laws, customs and language. Wales didn't have a king, but instead each region or area was controlled by a chief or prince.

King William of England wasn't very interested in conquering Wales, but he did worry about the Welsh attacking England! So he gave some of his most trusted barons land along the Welsh border and told them to make England safe from attack. So the barons built castles to stop the Welsh getting into England. As time went on, some of the English barons attacked the Welsh and took some of their land. By 1247, the English had captured most of Wales, except for a mountainous area in the north (see **Source A**).

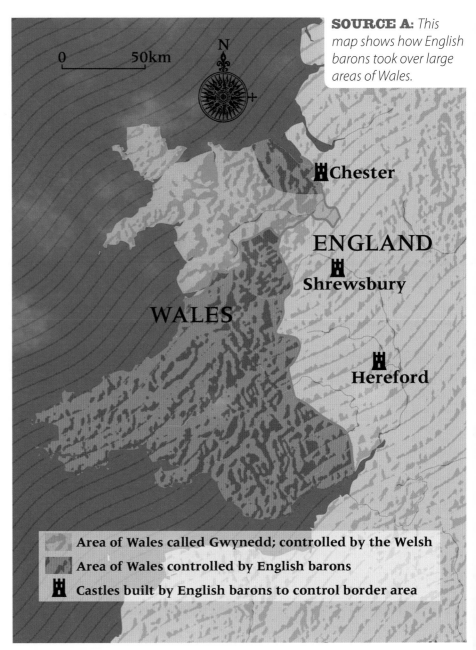

SOURCE A: This map shows how English barons took over large areas of Wales.

Chester

ENGLAND

Shrewsbury

WALES

Hereford

0   50km

N

	Area of Wales called Gwynedd; controlled by the Welsh
	Area of Wales controlled by English barons
🏰	Castles built by English barons to control border area

The Welsh fight back

From 1247 onwards, the Welsh began to fight back more fiercely against the English and take back some of their land. The Welsh were led by a man called Llywelyn, who called himself 'Prince of Wales' (see **Source B**).

A new English king

In 1272, Edward I became king of England – and he didn't like the growing power of Llywelyn and the Welsh. So the English king told Llywelyn that he must promise to be loyal to him and accept him as his ruler. Llywelyn refused so Edward attacked Wales and took back lots of land.

Edward wins

Llywelyn survived Edward's attack on Wales and soon rebelled again. Once more Edward's army invaded Wales, but this time Llywelyn was killed. His head was stuck on a pole outside the Tower of London.

Edward's 'Iron Ring'

Edward wanted to make sure that the Welsh didn't rebel again. So he built lots of large, stone castles throughout Wales to keep them under control. These castles, and the towns near to them, were filled with Englishmen, and were known as the 'Iron Ring'. By 1274, Wales was officially under English rule... and it is still part of Britain today.

Prince of Wales

King Edward introduced a new tradition too. In 1301 he gave his son the title 'Prince of Wales' so that no Welshman could claim the title for himself. Ever since, the eldest son of a British king or queen is given this title.

SOURCE B:
Llywelyn, pictured here, was known by some as 'Llywelyn the Great'.

SOURCE C: *The set of huge, new castles Edward built in the north of Wales was known as the 'Ring of Iron'.*

> **Hungry for More?**

One of Wales's most famous castles is Beaumaris in Anglesey (see **Source C**). However, Beaumaris was never finished! Find out about the construction of the castle… and why it wasn't completed.

Work

1 In what way is each of these dates important in the history of England versus Wales'?
   • 1066   • 1247   • 1272   • 1277   • 1284   • 1301

2 a What was Edward I's 'Ring of Iron'?
   b Why do you think Edward chose to build his strongest castles in the north of Wales?

3 Can you think of reasons why Edward's decision to make his young son 'Prince of Wales' might be:
   a hated by the Welsh?
   b liked by the Welsh?

In the early Middle Ages, Scotland was ruled by its own kings and was a separate country from England… but all that changed in 1286!

Mission Objectives

- Identify how and why England tried to conquer Scotland.
- Judge how successful these attempts were.

The king dies

In 1286 Scotland's king, Alexander III, died in a riding accident. He had no clear heir to take his place. Thirteen Scotsmen all wanted to be king, so the Scots asked the King of England (Edward I) to choose for them. In 1292, Edward picked a man named John Balliol, a distant relative of a past king of Scotland, to be king. However, Edward forced Balliol to make a promise. Balliol was allowed to be king, but he was told he had to obey Edward at all times. Balliol agreed… but changed his mind once he was crowned – he wanted complete control of Scotland!

Scotland is attacked

Edward was furious that Balliol refused to obey him, so he decided to teach him a lesson. In 1296, Edward gathered a massive army in Newcastle, in the north of England, and marched into Scotland. The Scottish warriors were beaten and Balliol was thrown into prison. Like Wales, Scotland was now controlled by the King of England (see **Sources B** and **C**).

Scottish rebellion

However, when Edward returned to England the Scots rose up in **rebellion**. Their new leader was William Wallace and they defeated the English in a famous battle at Stirling Bridge in 1297. Wallace skinned one of the men he killed and turned his skin into a sword belt. Edward returned to Scotland the following year and defeated the Scots at the Battle of Falkirk. Wallace was captured in 1305 and suffered the terrible fate of death by hanging, drawing and quartering. His head was put on a spike on London Bridge. An arm and a leg were each sent to Perth, Stirling, Newcastle and Berwick.

A new leader

In 1306, the Scots found a new leader in Robert the Bruce. Edward once again marched north to invade Scotland, but he died on the journey. He was 68 years old and left clear instructions as to what he wanted written on his grave. His tomb in Westminster Abbey in London reads, 'Here is Edward I, the Hammer of the Scots: keep my faith'.

King Edward's son was also called Edward. He was crowned King Edward II in 1307. He wasn't a particularly good soldier and Robert the Bruce took full advantage of this. In June 1314, Edward II sent a huge army of around 25,000 men to Scotland to fight Robert and his army of 7000. At Bannockburn the Scots defeated the English in just two days.

Robert the Bruce remained King of Scotland whilst Edward II and his battered and bruised army returned to England. Scotland remained a separate country, not tied to England at all, for the next 300 years.

FACT!

You will notice a lot of King Edwards and Richards and Henrys during your studies this year. Similar to today, people in the Middle Ages liked to name their children after relatives, and often, after themselves. So, King Edward named his son Edward, who became King Edward II after his father died… and who named his son Edward too!

SOURCE A: *Edward I named himself 'the Hammer of the Scots'.*

'You seized my castles and land without any excuse. You robbed me and my subjects. You took Scotsmen off to England to be prisoners in your castles. Things just go from bad to worse. Now you have crossed the border with a great army and have started killing and burning.'

▲ **SOURCE B:** *Part of a letter from John Balliol to Edward I in 1296.*

'John Balliol, the King of Scotland, promised to obey me. Then he and some of his nobles began a plot against me. English ships that were in Scottish ports were burned, and the sailors were killed. An army of Scots invaded England. They burned villages, monasteries and churches. In one place, they set fire to a school with the children still in it. I could stand it no more. So I declared war and invaded Scotland.'

▲ **SOURCE C:** *Part of a letter from Edward I to the Pope in 1301, explaining his actions.*

Hungry for More?

Mel Gibson played William Wallace in the film *Braveheart*. Some historians criticized the film because they said it wasn't true to life. Try to find out what parts of the story were changed and what was added.

FACT!

In 1296, Edward stole the 'Stone of Destiny', an ancient rectangular block of stone on which Scottish kings sat when they were crowned. The stone was taken to London and made part of a specially built throne on which *English* kings and queens were then crowned. In 1996, the stone was returned to Scotland. However, it will be returned to London every time a new British monarch is crowned.

Work

1 a Look at **Source B**. What can we learn about how Edward treated the Scottish from this source?
   b Look at **Source C**. What does this source tell us about Edward's reasons for invading Scotland?

2 Create a timeline covering 150 years, from 1200 to 1350. On your timeline, add the key events (with a short explanation) in the relationship between England and Scotland at this time.

England and its neighbours: Ireland

During the Middle Ages, England fought many wars against its neighbours – the Welsh, the Scots, and the French – in an attempt to conquer their countries. Sometimes the wars were successful and England took over large parts of these countries for a long time. Sometimes, however, the English were beaten and driven out. But what about Ireland? Did English kings try to control Ireland too?

Mission Objectives

- Analyse how the English tried to control Ireland.
- Assess why medieval kings failed to conquer Ireland.

Medieval Ireland

At the beginning of the Middle Ages, Ireland was divided up into several small kingdoms. There was no single ruler and rival Irish kings or chiefs fought each other for control of the different areas. It had been like this for centuries. Sometimes the Vikings invaded Ireland – some Vikings even managed to settle in Ireland and set up small villages.

The English kings get involved

Some of the early Norman kings (like William the Conqueror and Henry I) showed no interest in conquering Ireland. The Irish Sea was rough and difficult for boats to cross. In addition, Ireland wasn't a particularly rich country so the English felt they wouldn't gain much from taking it over.

But in 1166, the Irish leader of an area called Leinster asked King Henry II of England for help. His name was Dermot MacMurrough and he was busy fighting the leader of another Irish kingdom. Henry sent English barons to help… but they just took Irish land for themselves, and within a few years, English barons controlled more land in Ireland than the Irish! Henry II even visited Ireland and declared himself its 'overlord'. Eventually, the Irish kings accepted Henry's rule and agreed to obey him (see **Source B**).

English control weakens

But English kings didn't really have true control over Ireland. It was too far away, and the Irish often attacked the English settlements in Ireland. King John built castles there to try to protect the English settlers and control the Irish… but this didn't work particularly well either (see **Source D**).

The English kings Edward II and Richard II made attempts to conquer Ireland, but with little success. By the end of the Middle Ages, English power in Ireland had shrunk to a small area around Dublin. This was called 'the Pale' and had to be defended with castles, high walls and ditches. Some English settlers married into Irish families, took Irish names and adopted Irish ways. Scottish settlers moved into the northern part of Ireland too.

FACT!

The area of Ireland called 'the Pale' was heavily fortified. 'Beyond the Pale' is a saying that is still used today to describe something that is completely uncivilized or uncontrollable.

What Happened When?

1492

The English struggles in Ireland are an early example of the English trying to explore and increase the number of places they control and trade with. This really kicked off in 1492, when Christopher Columbus discovered the 'New World' of America.

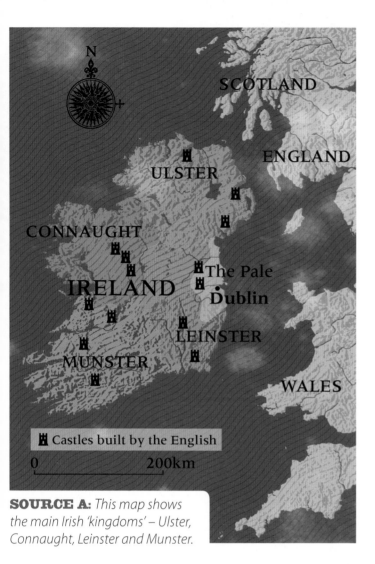

SOURCE A: *This map shows the main Irish 'kingdoms' – Ulster, Connaught, Leinster and Munster.*

Castles built by the English

0   200km

'When the Irish understood that King Henry only meant peace and that he wished to bring law and order to Ireland, they met him to discuss peace. Since they had trouble keeping peace amongst themselves, they handed power over to Henry II so that they should have peace.'

▲ **SOURCE B:** *This account was written by an English monk in 1172.*

Be a Top Historian

Top historians don't just study their own country. It's important to study the **relationships** between countries and how these have **changed** over time.

'The Irish have become wicked through mixing with the English. Different from us in language and customs, all hope of staying peaceful with them is out of the question.'

▲ **SOURCE C:** *The Irish chiefs and kings sent a letter to the Pope in 1317, explaining why they couldn't get on with the English settlers.*

SOURCE D: *King John's castle in Limerick, Ireland, was built around 1200.*

Work

1 Look at **Source B**.
   a According to this source, why did King Henry II go to Ireland?
   b Why did the Irish kings accept him?
2 Compare **Sources B** and **C**.
   a How had the Irish attitude to the English changed?
   b Can you suggest reasons why this change in attitude happened?

9.4A Why do we give the 'V sign' as an insult?

Most people know what the 'V sign' is! It is usually when a person puts two fingers up at someone in order to insult them. Believe it or not, people have been sticking up two fingers as an insult for around 700 years. Legend has it that it all started during the Hundred Years War – a long series of battles between England and France that began in 1337. So how did the fighting start? Did the fighting last for exactly one hundred years? Which country finally came out on top? And how is the V sign insult linked to it all?

Mission Objectives

- Identify the causes of the Hundred Years War.
- Summarize the key events of the Hundred Years War.
- Discover how one of Britain's best-known insults reputedly has its origins in the Hundred Years War.

Reasons for war

In 1337, the King of England was Edward III. He was 24 years old and determined to be a stronger ruler than his father, Edward II. The young king enjoyed fighting and viewed a war with France as a way of achieving glory on the battlefield. But there were other reasons why war broke out too:

- England controlled large areas of France (see **Source A**). One of these areas was where a lot of wine was made. When the wine was brought over to England it was taxed, and King Edward made lots of money from this. However, the French threatened to take over this wine-producing area.

- England sold lots of wool abroad. Areas near France (for example, Flanders – see **Source A**) turned this wool into cloth. Both the English and the people in places like Flanders made lots of money doing this. But the French threatened to take over these areas. If the wool trade was stopped it would make England poorer… and people wouldn't be able to afford to pay King Edward as much tax.

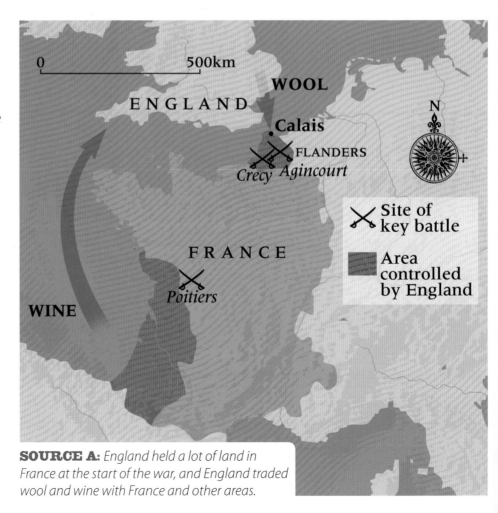

SOURCE A: *England held a lot of land in France at the start of the war, and England traded wool and wine with France and other areas.*

There were other reasons why war broke out too:

- Edward III was closely linked to France. His grandfather had been King of France and his mother was the daughter of a French king. He thought he had a better claim to the throne of France than the actual French king at the time, Philip VI.

- Edward was trying to conquer Scotland at the same time. The French promised to help the Scots, which made Edward furious!

Fighting the French

In 1337, England and France started fighting. There were battles at sea, but most of the fighting was done on French land. None of the fighting happened in England. The Hundred Years War features one of the most legendary victories in military history, where 10,000 English soldiers beat around 40,000 Frenchmen at the Battle of Agincourt. The war lasted, off and on, until 1453 – a total of 116 years. However, historians chose to call it 'the Hundred Years War', which sounds a bit better than 'the One Hundred and Sixteen Years War'!

SOURCE B: *This picture shows Henry V leading the English to victory at the Battle of Agincourt.*

Be a Top Historian

Top historians try to judge whether they think some causes of an event are more important (or **significant**) than others. Sometimes they try to put them in order of importance (or **significance**). (See Work activity **1b**.)

Work

1   a   Create a spider diagram that shows each of the causes of the Hundred Years War.
    b   Number the causes on your spider diagram in order of importance – the cause you think was the most significant should be number 1, and so on.
    c   Compare your order of causes with a partner's order. Do you agree or disagree? Explain your reasoning to each other.

2   Imagine you've been asked to write a short article for a new website on the Hundred Years War. The paragraph is entitled, 'What caused the Hundred Years War and your editor has allowed you 150 words for your paragraph. Hand write or type up your article.

Why do we give the 'V sign' as an insult?

Roller coaster ride

Like most wars, the Hundred Years War was a bit of a roller coaster with its ups and downs. First one side did well and was on the up, and then the other side did well, and so on. Read the roller coaster story of the war carefully.

1356

English victories continue at the Battle of Poitiers, led by Edward's son, the Black Prince. Philip VI was captured and held to ransom for £500,000. That's five times more than Edward normally earned in a year!

1347

Edward makes it a hat-trick of victories by capturing the French port of Calais. This is the closest port to England and was to remain in English hands for over 200 years.

1346

Edward enjoys another clear victory on land. At the Battle of Crécy, his 12,000 archers and 2400 knights smash 12,000 French knights, 6000 crossbowmen and 20,000 militiamen. The English archers prove that they are far superior to the crossbowmen.

1340

England wins the Battle of Sluys. The English surprise the French ships while they are anchored. Although the battle takes place at sea, it is fought by soldiers jumping from ship to ship fighting as if they are on land. The French defeat means England controls the Channel and can invade France whenever it feels like it.

Winning battles... but losing the war

Despite famous victories at Sluys, Crécy, Poitiers, and Agincourt, the English armies were never strong enough to defeat the French once and for all. By 1453, the French had pushed the English out of France almost completely. All England had left was the port of Calais.

The 'V sign'

Now back to the question of why the V sign is used as an insult. The answer lies in the fact that the English archers, who shot their arrows so brilliantly, were greatly feared by the French. A good English archer could fire ten arrows a minute and kill a man up to 200 metres away. At the Battle of Crécy, King Edward's archers shot 72,000 arrows in 90 seconds, killing thousands.

So, if an English archer was captured, the French would cut off the first two fingers of his hand. Can you think why? And in response to this, some English archers, when they saw a captured Frenchman, would run up to him and stick up their two fingers to show that they were still a threat! Over time this gesture became known as an insult.

Be a Top Historian

Top historians can spot what are known as 'turning points' in history. These are key events that **changed** things completely. Can you spot any key turning points in the Hundred Years War?

1370
The French start to fight back and, when the Black Prince falls ill, they win back some of their land.

1415
The new English king, Henry V, decides to renew the English claim to the French throne. He invades France and wins a famous victory at Agincourt. The French king lets Henry marry his daughter, and agrees that Henry should be the next King of France when he dies.

1377
The Black Prince dies in 1376 and his father dies the following year.

The French take advantage of the lack of English leaders and use cannons to recapture English castles in France.

1422
Disaster! Henry V dies before becoming king of both England and France! His son is only nine months old and the French strike back under the leadership of a 17-year-old peasant girl called Joan of Arc. (Find out more about her on pages 152 and 153.)

1453
The French regain all their land except for the tiny area around Calais.

Work

1 a How many years did the Hundred Years War last?
   b Why do you think it got its nickname?

2 What are the origins of the 'V sign' insult? Explain your answer.

3   **The Big Write!**

You are part of a group that is going to make the story of the Hundred Years War into a film. You must 'pitch' the idea to a Hollywood film studio to get the money you need to make the film. You will have a short amount of time (one to two minutes) to explain to a group of Hollywood businesspeople why the Hundred Years War would be a good subject for a film and why people should be told about it. Plan and write your pitch. You might want to storyboard the film too… and decide who plays who!

In the 1420s, during the Hundred Years War, England was on the verge of conquering the whole of France. But that all changed when a 16-year-old peasant girl went to see the French king and persuaded him to let her lead one of his armies! So what on earth made the French put a young girl in charge of an army? What made her such a good leader? And what happened to the greatest heroine in French history?

Mission Objectives

- Recall who Joan of Arc was and how she affected the outcome of the Hundred Years War.
- Examine why she is still a national hero in France today.

1 Joan was born in Domrémy around 1412. At the age of 12, she claimed that Saint Catherine, Saint Margaret and Saint Michael 'visited' her and told her to attend church regularly.

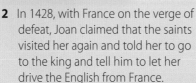

2 In 1428, with France on the verge of defeat, Joan claimed that the saints visited her again and told her to go to the king and tell him to let her drive the English from France.

3 Joan saw the desperate French king, who had been praying for a miracle. She told him that she knew he had asked God to save the French people from suffering. The king was amazed! He hadn't told anybody about his prayers – she must have spoken to God!

4 Joan was questioned about her visions by a panel of holy men for three weeks. They told the king that she must be telling the truth and to put her in charge of one of his armies!

6 Joan led an attack on the English. Despite being injured, she inspired the French to victory! Soon, the English armies were being pushed back by the French. Never again would the English control so much of France.

5 Joan believed it was God's wish for her to go to Orléans, which was being attacked by the English. She wore a suit of armour and immediately made the soldiers go to church, give up swearing and stop stealing. People said she was sent by God and men flocked to fight for her.

7 Joan continued to lead the French to victory in other battles. When the new French king was crowned, Joan stood next to him, carrying her banner.

9 Joan was put on trial by the Church for being a witch but there was not enough evidence. In the end, they found her guilty of dressing as a man, which was against church law, she was burned at the stake!

8 Joan continued to fight for France but was betrayed. She was captured at the town of Compiègne and sold to the English. The French were devastated; the English were overjoyed!

SOURCE A: *This statue of Joan of Arc is in the centre of Paris. She is still greatly admired by French people today.*

FACT!

Twenty-five years after her death, the Church said that Joan of Arc should never have been killed and that she was not a witch. In 1920 she was made a saint after French soldiers in World War One reported miracles after praying to her.

Joan of Arc's revenge!

Soon after Joan's execution, people on both sides started to believe it was a mistake. Even while Joan was burning, an English onlooker is said to have cried out, 'We are lost, for we have burned a saint.' The King of England's own secretary hurried back from the execution and said, 'We are all ruined, for a good and holy person was burned.' By 1453, England had lost all of its land in France apart from a tiny area around Calais.

Work

1 Describe ways in which Joan of Arc was different from the kind of people who usually led armies in the Middle Ages.

2 Why do you think so many people followed Joan into battle?

3 Why do you think that Joan of Arc is such a heroine in France today?

4 You have been asked to contribute to a children's history book called *Who's Who in French History*. You are to write the entry for Joan of Arc but have been told there's only enough room for five sentences! Write the five sentences for inclusion in the book.

Choose your weapons!

Medieval warfare was a horrific experience. Archers and crossbowmen could stand 150–250 metres away from their enemy and fire arrows or crossbow bolts with savage accuracy. But sometimes soldiers would have to get close to each other and fight hand-to-hand. As a result, you'd be close enough to the man you were fighting to smell the fear on his breath. You would feel your weapon slice through his flesh and crunch through his bones. At any moment, you could lose an arm or a leg or be stabbed straight through the chest and left to die an agonizing death on the battlefield. Improvements and changes in technology saw a variety of weapons used in the Middle Ages. Study these pages – and choose your weapons!

Mission Objectives

- Identify different weapons that were used in medieval warfare.
- Judge which weapons were the most effective and explain why.

Ⓐ English longbow
One of the deadliest weapons on the battlefield, the longbow could be fired from over 200 metres away. It was around six feet long and made from wood with a linen string. Several English kings introduced laws that made it compulsory for men to practise archery.

Ⓑ Crossbow
Crossbows were mini wooden catapults used to fire bolts through armour at a range of over 100 metres. They were easier to use than longbows, but couldn't fire as far.

Ⓒ Mace
In around 1300, the mace started to be used more often. This was a heavy metal club with short, thick blades – or flanges. It was brought crashing down onto opponents, shattering bones and crushing skulls

Ⓓ Caltrop
These iron spikes were thrown on the ground and stabbed through the feet of charging horses and men.

E Pike

One of the most basic weapons on the battlefield, pikes (long sticks tipped with steel) were perfect for footsoldiers facing knights on horseback. Charging knights would be brought to the ground by large groups of pike-wielding men who stabbed the horses.

F Battleaxe

Battleaxes were devastating weapons that could slice a man in half with a single blow. A lot of space was needed to swing them, though, and they had to be held in both hands.

G Flail

Flails appeared in around 1500. Because of the chain they could be swung much faster and with much greater force than a mace. They were often used to stick into armour and drag knights from their horses.

H Gunpowder

Gunpowder was used in China way back in the ninth century AD, but it wasn't until the fourteenth century that it was used as a weapon in Europe! At first, cannons were used to fire large metal balls at an enemy – but they weren't very accurate. Things did improve, though, and handguns started to appear on the battlefield by the fifteenth century. Although useful for scaring horses, guns and cannon didn't become really effective until the very end of the Middle Ages.

I Swords and daggers

At the beginning of the Middle Ages, swords were large chopping weapons with a razor-sharp double-edged blade. As armour became stronger, shorter swords with extremely sharp points became more popular. Many men also chose to take a small dagger with them into battle. It came in useful when things got up close and personal and was often used to finish opponents off!

Work

1 Explain which two weapons you would choose if you were fighting a knight on horseback.

2 Why do you think guns weren't used more often on the medieval battlefield?

3 **EITHER:** Draw a medieval knight or footsoldier carrying the weapons you would choose to take onto the battlefield (a maximum of three). Label your picture, clearly showing the names of the weapons and explaining why you have chosen them.

OR: Imagine you own a medieval weapons shop. Design a website (on paper) that describes the weapons you sell and why they would be useful in battle. Look at the website homepage on page 56 for an example of how a website could be structured.

What were the Wars of the Roses?

Families can be very complicated. They can be very large and full of people of different ages and personalities. Sometimes certain people in the family don't get on with each other – and there are often step-parents and half-brothers and sisters to deal with too! Also, families usually have different 'sides' to them. There's often a 'mother's side' and a 'father's side', which have different surnames. And sometimes one side might fall out with the other side.

A right royal row

Don't think for a minute that royal families are any different to ordinary families when it comes to falling out with each other. Throughout history, kings have argued (and even fought) with brothers, half-brothers, cousins, wives, and sons. Edward II, for example, was murdered on the orders of his own wife so that their son could be king. And Richard II was put in prison and starved to death by his cousin. The cousin then became King Henry IV!

Lancasters and Yorks

In the early 1400s, members of England's royal family began arguing amongst themselves over who should be king. The argument involved two different sides of the same family – the York side and the Lancaster side. Both sides of the family were directly related to King Edward III (who ruled England between 1327 and 1377) and both felt they had good reason to rule.

The argument began when Henry VI was King of England. Henry was from the Lancaster side of the family. He was a gentle, religious man who struggled to control the country – and he was a poor military leader too. Tragically, he also suffered from bouts of madness and memory loss, and would sit silently for hours on end in a dark room.

An opportunity for the Yorks

During one of Henry's bouts of insanity, a distant relative from the other side of the family (the Yorks) was chosen to be England's 'Protector' in Henry's place. His name was Richard, Duke of York, and he ruled England until Henry recovered.

When Henry was well again, Richard lost his power… but he wanted it back! So, he gathered an army to fight King Henry. Henry was beaten and Richard became 'Protector' again. Henry was forced into hiding but his wife, Margaret, gathered her own army and beat the Yorks. Richard was killed and Henry was now in control again.

However, Richard's son, Edward, was devastated by his father's death and swore revenge. And so began a series of violent and bloody battles between two sides of the same family – Edward and the Yorks versus Henry and the Lancasters.

FACT!

The fighting between the York family and the Lancaster family later became known as the Wars of the Roses. This is because the two families chose different coloured roses as emblems for their shields and banners. The Lancasters chose a red rose and the Yorks chose a white one.

The Wars of the Roses

The two sides fought each other for over 30 years. First one side would win a battle and choose a king to rule the country, then the other side would win and choose their own king. **Source B** shows how each side won lots of different battles.

Hungry for More?

The Lancaster and York families fought many battles with each side winning their fair share. Pick a battle from the map below. Research it, using the library and the Internet, and produce a brief fact file on it.

SOURCE A: *King Henry VI came from the House of Lancaster.*

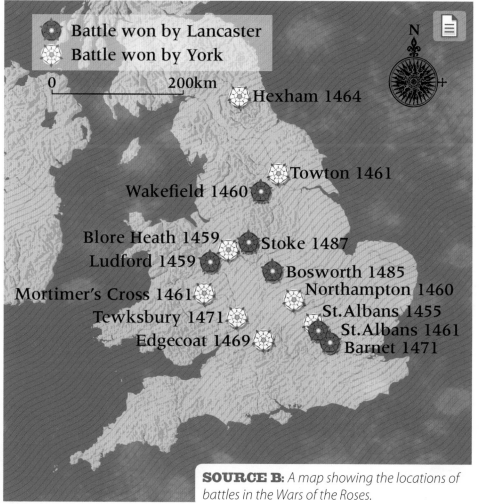

Battle won by Lancaster
Battle won by York

0   200km

N

Hexham 1464

Towton 1461

Wakefield 1460

Blore Heath 1459   Stoke 1487
Ludford 1459

Bosworth 1485
Mortimer's Cross 1461   Northampton 1460
Tewksbury 1471   St.Albans 1455
St.Albans 1461
Edgecoat 1469   Barnet 1471

SOURCE B: *A map showing the locations of battles in the Wars of the Roses.*

Work

1   a   Who were the Lancasters?
    b   Who were the Yorks?
    c   How did the Wars of the Roses get their name?
    d   According to the map (**Source B**), how many battles made up the Wars of the Roses?

2   In your own words, explain the role played by each of the following people during the Wars of the Roses:
    a   Henry VI
    b   Richard, Duke of York
    c   Margaret of Anjou, Henry VI's wife
    d   Edward, Richard of York's son

All change

As a result of each side winning different battles, the throne changed hands many times. Look at the diagram below. It illustrates how the job of 'King of England' swapped between the York family and the Lancaster family during the period known as the Wars of the Roses.

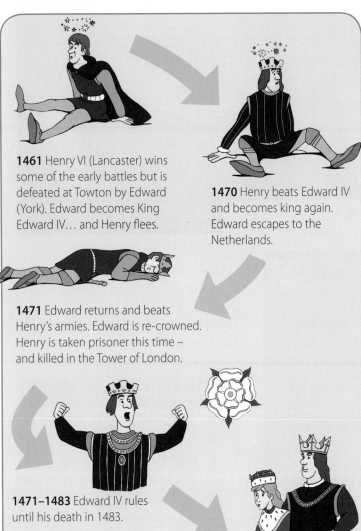

1461 Henry VI (Lancaster) wins some of the early battles but is defeated at Towton by Edward (York). Edward becomes King Edward IV… and Henry flees.

1470 Henry beats Edward IV and becomes king again. Edward escapes to the Netherlands.

1471 Edward returns and beats Henry's armies. Edward is re-crowned. Henry is taken prisoner this time – and killed in the Tower of London.

1471–1483 Edward IV rules until his death in 1483.

1483 After Edward's death, his brother becomes King Richard III.

1485 The last important member of the Lancaster family challenges Richard III for the crown. His name is Henry Tudor (Henry VI was his half-uncle). At the Battle of Bosworth Field, Henry Tudor and his Lancaster supporters beat Richard III and the Yorks. Henry Tudor becomes King Henry VII – the first Tudor king.

SOURCE A: *Edward IV was king from 1461 until 1483.*

So what happens next?

Most people thought Henry VII – who was a Lancaster – would soon be attacked and killed by supporters of the York family. But Henry held onto the throne and went on to rule England well. One reason why Henry was able to do this was because he cleverly married Edward IV's daughter, Elizabeth! This meant that the king was from the Lancaster family and the queen was from the York family, so their children would be both Yorks *and* Lancasters (see **Source C**). The marriage united the two families and ended the wars. The new king even united the York and Lancaster roses to create a new national symbol – the Tudor rose! (See **Source B**.)

SOURCE B: *The Tudor rose is a combination of the roses of Lancaster and York.*

SOURCE C: *This double portrait of Elizabeth of York and Henry VII shows the red and white roses of Lancaster and York uniting because of their marriage.*

SOURCE D: *The Tudor rose can still be seen today in all sorts of places. You probably didn't realize that there are ten of them on the England football badge.*

FACT!

King Richard III's bones were found in 2012, buried underneath a car park which was built on the site of an old church. The bones showed that Richard suffered from a crooked spine and was probably killed by a heavy blow to the head (the back of his skull was sliced off). There were eight wounds on his skull in total. Analysis of the soil around the body showed that he probably suffered from ringworm (a parasite that gets inside your body).

Work

1 Copy out and complete the sentences below. You will find the words in the box, but some words won't fit!

The Wars of the _____ is the name given to a series of _____ for the English. The wars were fought between two families, the _____ and the Yorks. Over the years, depending on which family was winning, the throne changed hands many times. The _____ who ruled as king during the majority of the wars were _____ VI (from the Lancaster family) and _____ IV (from the _____ family).

Henry	chair	Lancasters	York
Roses	battles	Daffodils	throne
women	Edward	Richard	men

2 **a** Who was Henry Tudor?
  b Which battle did Henry Tudor win?
  c Which king did Henry Tudor defeat?
  d After Henry Tudor was crowned King Henry VII, how did he end the fighting between the families of York and Lancaster?

3 In 2012, researchers found the body of King Richard III, the York king killed at the Battle of Bosworth by Henry Tudor's army in 1485. This renewed interest in the Wars of the Roses and there were many news reports on the wars on TV. Imagine you've been asked to produce a short report for a children's news programme on the Wars of the Roses. The report is scheduled to last no more than 60 seconds and must contain everything a young historian would need to know.

9.8A The Princes in the Tower

You are about to learn about one of history's greatest mysteries. This fascinating 'whodunnit' has had historians baffled for over 500 years. When you have looked at the evidence, see if you can draw any conclusions.

Edward IV loved drinking, dancing and hunting. Most of all he loved eating. After one huge meal in April 1483, he was so full that he went to bed for hours. He caught a fever there and died. His son, also called Edward, travelled to London to be crowned. His other son, Richard, was due to join them later. Prince Edward was twelve years old and Prince Richard was nine.

The two boys stayed in the Tower of London while Prince Edward prepared for his **coronation**. The boys' uncle, also called Richard, had been asked to look after the princes and help young Edward until he could rule the country on his own.

In June, a rumour started to spread across London. People were saying that young Prince Edward's father had not been married to his mother. This meant that Prince Edward couldn't become king. The Bishop of Bath and Wells said that the rumours were true, so two weeks later Prince Edward's uncle, Richard, was crowned king instead. He became King Richard III.

But what about the two boys? In the summer of 1483, they were seen playing in the gardens of the Tower of London. After that, they were never seen again. What had happened to them? Could they have been murdered? If so, who did it? The History Mystery detectives need to investigate!

SOURCE A: This painting was created long after the princes were alive. It is one artist's interpretation of how the princes might have looked.

Evidence A

Written in 1483 by an Italian who was visiting London. The writer's English was very poor and the book he wrote on Richard was full of factual mistakes.

'Prince Edward and his brother were taken to the inner rooms of the tower, and day by day began to be seen less behind the bars and the windows, until they stopped appearing altogether.'

Evidence B

A speech made by a Frenchman in 1484.

'Look at what has happened since the death of King Edward IV. His courageous children have been killed and the crown has gone to their murderer.'

Evidence C

Written in The Great Chronicle of London, *1512.*

'The children were seen shooting and playing in the garden until Easter [1484]. After Easter there was much whispering among the people that the king had put the children to death.'

Evidence D

Written in 1513 by Sir Thomas More. More was brought up by John Morton, a man who hated Richard III because he put him in prison in 1483.

'King Richard wanted Sir James Tyrrell to carry out his wishes. Tyrrell decided that the princes should be murdered in their beds. He picked Miles Forrest and John Dighton to do the job.

About midnight Forrest and Dighton entered the room where the children lay in their beds and forced the feather bed and pillows hard into their mouths until they stopped breathing.

They laid their bodies out naked on the bed and fetched Sir James to see them. Then he got the murderers to bury them at the bottom of the stairs, deep in the ground under a heap of stones. Later a priest dug up the bodies and moved them to a place which only he knew.'

Wise Up Words

coronation

Evidence E

In 1674, some workmen were working on a staircase in the Tower of London. Two metres underground they discovered a box full of bones. The bones were reburied in Westminster Abbey. They are still there today.

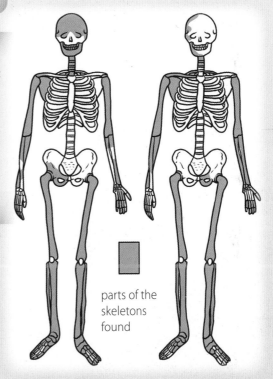

SOURCE B: *This painting is from the twentieth century, and also is an artist's interpretation of what happened to the princes.*

Evidence F

From a website by a modern historian.

'When the bones were discovered in 1674, Charles II, who was king at the time, placed them in a marble casket and gave them a full funeral. During the service, the Archbishop of London said this:

"It is right and meet that we commend the bones of these young princes to a place of final rest. Their fates at the order of Richard III grieves us, and though almost two centuries have passed, the vile deeds of that villain shall ne'er be forgotten."'

Evidence G

In 1933, two doctors examined the bones. Their report said that:

- the skeletons were not complete
- the bones belonged to two children aged about ten and twelve
- a stain on one of the skulls may mean that they could have been suffocated
- the bones could have been there since 1100
- the elder boy had a serious tooth disease.

Evidence H

In 1955, different doctors looked at the report made in 1933. They weren't allowed to look at the bones but studied pictures instead. They said that:

- the bones were from children younger than the two princes
- the stain was not caused by suffocation.

parts of the skeletons found

Hungry for More?

Carbon dating is a technique scientists use to find out how old something is. When the remains were examined in 1933, carbon dating was not available to the scientists, and in 1955 they only had photographs of the bones; they had to try and estimate how old things were by the way they looked. Do you think the bones should be re-examined so scientists can give us a better idea of the age of the bones? How would this help us decide if the bones are indeed those of the Princes in the Tower?

Work

Starting your investigation

Think about what you've learned so far:

1 What do **you** think happened to the princes?

2 What makes you think this? List the evidence that led you to this decision.

3 Do you trust all the evidence? Can you think of reasons why some of the things you've read so far might not be totally reliable?

History Mystery

9.8B The Princes in the Tower

A different story?

In 1485, King Richard III was killed in battle. He was beaten by a rival for the throne named Henry Tudor. Henry was crowned King of England and became Henry VII. Now it's time to look at more evidence.

Evidence I

By historian Philip Lindsay in 1933.
'Richard had no reason to kill them. Henry Tudor had every reason. If the princes lived they would have more right to be king than Henry Tudor. Henry spread the word that Richard had done the killing.'

Evidence J

There were many rumours at the time. Some said that the two boys had fallen off a bridge. Others said that Prince Edward had become ill and died naturally and that Prince Richard was secretly taken abroad and lived for years afterwards. Later, there were people who pretended to be Richard, but none pretended to be Prince Edward.

Evidence K

Written by a modern historian.
'When Henry Tudor became king, he gave land and important jobs to James Tyrrell, John Dighton and Miles Forrest.'

SOURCE C: *Henry VII would never have become king had the boys survived.*

Evidence J

If Richard had killed the boys, all he had to do was display their bodies and say they died of a fever. But he didn't, and he didn't because they were still alive. But when Henry became king he had to get rid of them. Henry had to hide the facts and when and where they died. Henry's whole case depended on no one knowing what exactly happened to the boys.

SOURCE D: *Richard III, the man who was king when the boys disappeared.*

Evidence L

This family tree shows how both Henry VII and Richard III benefited from the disappearance of the two princes. With both princes dead, King Richard III hoped to remain king for as long as he could. Also, Henry VII benefitted from the princes', deaths because Edward IV had no other male children, bringing Henry closer to the throne! Interestingly, Henry VII married the princes' sister, Elizabeth of York.

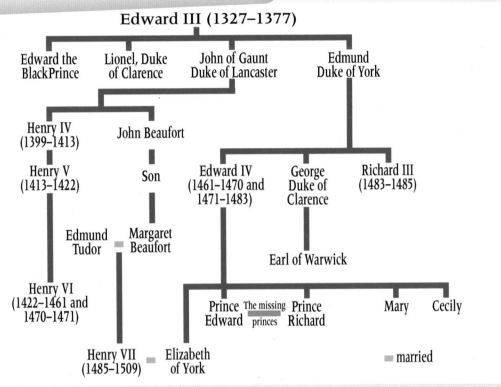

Work

Now it's time to try to solve this mystery. You need to look closely at all the evidence.

1 **Find out about the events leading up to the disappearance of the two princes.**

Think about where and when the princes were last seen. Why were they there?

2 **Find a motive – who might want them dead and why?**

Is there anybody who might benefit from the princes' deaths? Why are Richard III and Henry Tudor both suspects? Explain your ideas.

3 **Find any evidence to show it might not have been a murder.**

Perhaps the boys died of natural causes? Write down any ideas you have to support this theory.

4 **Find any evidence for murder.**

Is there any evidence to support the idea that the two princes were murdered? If so, how and by whom?

5 **Consider whose evidence might not be reliable.**

Could someone be making things up? Why might someone lie? Does any one piece of evidence contradict another? Write down your theories.

6 **Now make your decision.**

Write a short paragraph to explain what you think happened to the Princes in the Tower.

Was King Henry VII a gangster?

Stop and think: have you ever heard of a 'gangster'? Some of you will have. Take a moment to think and talk about what a gangster is and what the word means.

Mission Objectives

- Investigate the life of Henry VII.
- Assess the tactics Henry VII used to become more powerful.

A gangster is usually someone who is powerful. And they are often involved in unfair or criminal activities. They get money from people (sometimes unfairly) and make deals to increase their power. They often live lavish lifestyles and enjoy showing off their wealth and power. They sometimes even use weapons to bully people.

Now Henry VII was not a criminal: he was King of England and Wales. In 1485, when he was plain, old Henry Tudor, he had beaten King Richard III in the Battle of Bosworth Field, near Leicester. Richard was killed and Henry Tudor became the new king – Henry VII.

Henry VII, who had become king by fighting, was desperate to remain king. So he had to do things to keep his position safe. Now that you know what a gangster is, see if you think Henry VII acted like one.

He married a rival

Henry was a member of the Lancaster family. The Lancasters' bitter rivals were the members of the York family, who were also keen to rule the country. In 1486, Henry married a member of the rival family – Elizabeth of York. Now the Lancasters had a king and the Yorks had a queen.

He banned private armies

Some powerful men in England had their own private armies. Henry knew these armies could be used against him… so he made a law that banned them. One rich lord who failed to get rid of his private army was fined £10,000!

He made sure he had the best weapons

Cannons first appeared in Britain in the 1300s. They were the most destructive and feared weapons by the time Henry became king, so he made sure he had the finest cannons in the land.

He forced people to give him money

Henry made the rich people in his kingdom pay him heavy taxes. He sent ministers around the country looking for large, expensive houses. If they found one, the minister would force the owners to lend the king money (because they were obviously very rich). But Henry never paid the loan back.

He made deals with other countries

Henry once got Parliament to give him money to fight the French – then got the French king to pay him *not* to fight! He also made his eldest son, Arthur, marry a Spanish princess called Catherine of Aragon in order to become friendlier with Spain. And when Arthur died he said his youngest son, Henry, should marry her as well. He even encouraged his 18-year-old daughter (Mary) to marry the 52-year-old king of France, and his other daughter (Margaret) to marry the King of Scotland.

He made sure everyone knew he was king

Henry spent huge amounts of money on lavish parties and entertainment. The Tudor rose symbol appeared all over the country – in churches, paintings, palaces and cathedrals.

Henry dies

When Henry VII died in 1509, the throne was safe and England was at peace. He also left his son and heir, Henry, a fortune! But what do you think? Was Henry VII a bit of a gangster?

What Happened When? 1486

In 1486, the same year Henry VII married Elizabeth of York, the word 'football' was first used to describe a game where a ball is kicked (see pages 84 and 85).

SOURCE A: *A painting of Henry VII dating from 1505. He sent his picture to a possible new wife after his first wife, Elizabeth of York, died in 1503. Notice that he is clutching a rose in his right hand, one of the many Tudor symbols.*

Work

1 In your own words, explain what is meant by the word 'gangster'.

2 Imagine you are Henry VII and have been on the throne for several years. A new king in another country has written you a letter asking how you have become so powerful, raised so much money, and made yourself safe and secure. Write him a letter back.

3 Look again at your answer to question **1**. Do you think Henry VII acted like a gangster? Explain your opinion.

What does John know that Edwin didn't?

The world we live in is always changing. Sometimes small changes over a long period of time add up to large changes. Often a single invention, idea or discovery can have a huge impact on people and their way of life. For example, think how the invention of the Internet or the aeroplane has changed the way we live.

But sometimes things don't change a great deal. For example, the way some people worship God has remained unchanged for hundreds of years. But what about changes in the Middle Ages? If someone in early Tudor times could look back a few hundred years to 1100, would they think life had changed much, and what more would they know about the world?

Mission Objectives

- Examine some of the key discoveries, theories, ideas, and inventions of the Middle Ages.
- Assess how new ideas, theories, discoveries, and inventions changed Britain.

Meet Edwin, a man who lived around the time of the Norman Conquest, which started in 1066. Look below at what he thinks and believes about the world he lives in.

People in Europe, like me, know that Africa and Asia exist, but don't know much about them. Africa has hardly been explored by Europeans at all. There are rumours of faraway lands in the south and west... Explorers and traders go on long journeys over land or by sea. But travelling by sea can be dangerous because ships are so difficult to steer.

A long time ago, people thought the earth was flat... but not any more. We know the Earth is a globe, but aren't sure how big it is. The Earth is also the centre of the universe and all the planets, the sun and the stars move around us.

Most people can't read or write. Some rich children are taught by priests or monks, but books are still rare and expensive. They are usually written out by hand, in Latin, by monks — and it sometimes takes them a whole year to copy out a Bible.

Doctors say bad blood is a common cause of illness, meaning that your body is 'out of balance'. They will cut you to make you bleed, or attach leeches to you to suck out the 'bad blood'. Sometimes holes are drilled into a patient's head to get rid of a headache... but the patient often dies.

The king rules over everyone. His loyal friends help him rule the land and control different areas. Most people live in the countryside and farm the land. However, there aren't many large towns — only eight have a population of over 3000.

Edwin

Poor people make their own medicines from plants and herbs, or ask the local wise woman to make a special potion. There aren't many doctors — and they get their medical knowledge from books written by the Ancient Greeks or Romans.

Religion is a vital part of everyday life. Everyone goes to church and knows that God controls everything — bad harvests, good weather, births, deaths... it's all God's work (or the Devil's!).

War is very brutal and armies fight up close with swords and axes or charge at each other on horses. Some soldiers are trained to use bows that can fire arrows a long way. Castles are dotted all over the country too — barons and knights live in them.

Now you've met Edwin and got to know him a little, take a journey through some of the big ideas, new advances and major inventions and discoveries of the next 400 or so years.

1167
University of Oxford began to grow, here, men learned how to become doctors, priests and lawyers

1182
Simple compasses first used in Europe, making it easier for sailors to sail in the right direction

1180
Rudders used on ships so they could be steered better

1150
Paper-making introduced in Europe

1185
Windmills first used to grind grain into flour in Britain

1279
Glass mirrors brought back by Crusader knights who had been fighting in the Holy Land

1265
First Parliament meets; after this, more people began to have more say in how the country was run

1231
University of Cambridge founded

1280
Spinning wheel invented, which sped up cloth-making

1280
Mechanical clocks invented; they began to appear on big buildings so people didn't have to listen to church bells to find out the time

1282
Spectacles first used

Around 1300
Gunpowder (invented in China) first used in cannons

1300
Foods like sugar, lemons, and apricots and spices like ginger brought back by Crusaders from the Holy Land and became more common in Britain

Be a Top Historian

Top historians must understand **change and continuity**. This means that in any point in history, there are things that change and things that stay the same (known as 'continuity'). Can you think of something about Britain that hasn't changed at all in recent years? What about something that's changed a lot?

1500
London's population reached around 50,000 people. By this time, there were about 30 towns with a population of more than 5000 people, but most people still lived in the countryside

1492
Christopher Columbus, an Italian explorer, reached the 'new world' of the Americas whilst trying to find a new sea route to islands around India. In the years to follow, lots of countries will send explorers to the 'new world' of North and South America. These voyages of discovery will begin to change people's view of the world and bring new goods and knowledge to Europe

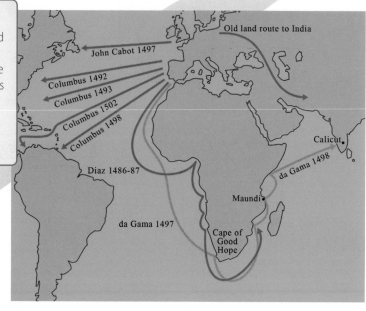

1477
William Caxton began printing books in Britain. Many of his books were printed in English, rather than Latin, so more people read them. By the late 1500s, around a third of the population could read

1464
Bamburgh Castle in Northumberland was the first castle in Britain to have its walls knocked down by cannon fire. Soon, lords and barons began to build castles for comfort rather than defence. Castles became smaller and were made from brick, with much thinner walls, more doors, and larger windows

1450
A German, Johannes Gutenberg, invented his printing press; books could be printed onto paper rather than copied out by monks. Books became cheaper and covered all sorts of subjects... so people began to read more and gain more knowledge

1326
Handguns first used; cannons and handguns changed the way battles were fought. Swords, axes, and bows and arrows were no match for guns and cannons: even castle walls could be knocked down easily

1450
The numbers 1 to 9 used in Britain; copied from the Arabic system used in Muslim countries

Now it's time to meet John, a gentleman who lived in the early 1500s, around the time Henry VII was King of England. Based on the new ideas, inventions and discoveries that are featured in the timeline and the rest of this book, discuss with a partner (or small groups) the answers to the questions dotted around John.

Is the king still in *complete* control of the country?

Have there been any major medical advances? What could this mean about the development of health and medicine?

How has warfare changed… and what has caused this change?

How has travelling by ship changed?

How has John's knowledge of the world changed (especially after 1492)?

Are books still as expensive as they were?

What new foods and ideas might John know about? And how would he know of them?

What new technology or inventions would John know about? How might these things have changed people's lives?

John

Have there been any developments in knowledge about the position of the earth in relation to the sun and other planets?

Choose an invention or discovery from the timeline. Research it carefully. Who invented it? When? Where? How? Was there a special reason for its invention or discovery? How has it developed? Is it still used today? If so, where?

Hungry for More?

Work

1 a Write down at least five things that Edwin might think about Britain, the world, science, or medicine.

b For each thing you've written down in part **a**, say whether you think someone living 400 to 500 years later (like John) would still think the same thing or whether they'd think differently. Write in full sentences and explain yourself clearly.

c Do you think *we* know all there is to know? Or are there lots of things we don't know or understand about the world, science, and medicine? Explain your answer.

2 Inventions change things. For example, the invention of the passenger aeroplane meant that we could travel further and faster than ever before. Think about the following inventions:
- the spinning wheel, for winding wool into threads
- gunpowder
- compasses and rudders for ships
- printed books

Write a few sentences about each invention, saying why each of them was important and how you think it might have helped to change things.

Glossary

Abbey A building where a community of monks or nuns lived

AD 'Anno domini'; used for dates after the birth of Jesus Christ

Ale An alcoholic drink similar to beer

Apothecary A person who prepared and sold medicines

Barber-surgeon Men who performed surgery and dentistry as well as cutting hair

Barbican The outer defensive tower of a castle, found above the drawbridge

Battering ram A heavy beam swung or rammed against a door to break it down

Battleaxe A large, broad-bladed weapon

Battlements The top of a castle wall with openings for archers to shoot through

BC 'Before Christ'; used for dates before the birth of Jesus Christ

Beaker people A European Bronze Age people who settled in Britain and made decorated pottery

Black Death A killer disease that wiped out millions of people across Europe

Bloodletting The practice of making someone bleed to help cure an illness

British Isles The group of islands including Britain, Ireland, the Isle of Man, the Orkney Islands, and the Shetland Islands

Bronze Age A period when weapons and tools were made of bronze; it came between the Stone Age and the Iron Age

Bubonic One of the two types of plague in Black Death; carried by fleas

Chain mail Flexible armour made of small metal rings linked together

Chancellor The most important position in England after the king; it involved sending out royal letters and charters

Charter A statement of a group of people's rights, written by the king or a lord

Chivalry The moral and social code followed by medieval knights

Chronicle A account of important historical events, most often written by a monk

Chronology The arrangement of dates or events in the order they happened, starting with the earliest

Church The collective name for Christians across England and the world

Coat of arms A distinctive design belonging to a knight or family, often used on shields, flags and clothing

Concentric castle A castle built with several walls of decreasing heights, so soldiers could shoot attackers more effectively

Conqueror A person who takes over a place or people, often by invasion

Consecrated When someone is officially given a position of religious responsibility and duty

Constable A man in charge of a group of watchmen

Coronation The ceremony of crowning a king or queen

Crusades A series of journeys made by Europeans to take the Holy Land back from Muslims in the Middle Ages

Curtain wall A strong wall around a castle that linked towers together

Doom painting A painting in a church designed to show people images of heaven and hell

Dowry Money that a bride's family give to her husband when she marries, or to a nunnery when she becomes a nun

Dubbed When a man is touched on the shoulder with a sword and becomes a knight

Dysentery A disease that causes terrible diarrhoea

Earldom The piece of land that was controlled by an earl

Evidence The facts or information that we have about a particular event, person or place

Excommunicated When someone has been officially excluded from the Christian Church

Export A product that is sold to another country

Feudal system A system developed by King William where each group of people owed loyalty to the group above, starting with villeins, knights, barons and ending with the king

Fyrd Warriors who fought for Harold at the battle of Hastings; they were numerous, but not very well trained

Garderobe A toilet in a medieval building

Great Council A group, including the king and his barons, that met to discuss how the country should be run

Guild A group of a certain type of craftsmen, with their own rules

Hauberk A full-length coat of chain mail

Heir The person who is next in line to become king or queen

Herald A person who supervised tournaments, made annoucements and carried messages

Heraldry The way in which coats of arms were created and used to identify knights or families

Housecarl A type of well trained warrior who used battleaxes and fought for Harold at the Battle of Hastings

Hue and cry A loud cry calling for people to pursue and capture a criminal

Humours The four main liquids in the body; illness was thought to be caused by them being out of balance

Hundred Years War A series of battles between England and France that began in 1337

Hunter-gatherer A person who lived mainly by hunting, fishing and harvesting wild plants

Illuminated A manuscript that is decorated with gold, silver and coloured designs

Immigrant Someone who has travelled from another country to settle

Inferior A person who is lower in rank or status than someone else

Infidel A person who has no religion or whose religion is not the same as that of another group of people

Inhabited A place where people live

Invasion Coming into another country, normally with an armed force, with the intention to take over

Iron Age A period when weapons and tools were made of iron; it came after the Bronze Age

Javelin A light spear thrown as a weapon

Jury A group of people who decide whether someone is innocent or guilty of a crime

Lance A long weapon with a pointed steel tip, used by warriors on horseback

Leech Blood-sucking creatures used in medieval medicine

Loyalty Staying true to someone, and being honest and helpful to them

Mace A heavy club with a spiked metal head that could break armour

Magna Carta A document setting out people's rights; the barons made King John sign it in 1215

Mangonel A device used in sieges that could throw stones and other objects

Manuscript A book that was written by hand, often by monks, and was sometimes illuminated

Marshal A man responsible for supervising tournaments and making sure competitors didn't cheat

Massacred When a large group of people has been brutally killed by someone else

Merchant A person who is involved in the buying and selling of goods

Minstrel A medieval singer or musician who often sang tales of heroic deeds

Miracle play A popular medieval play based on biblical stories or the lives of the saints

Monastery A building where a community of monks lived

Monk A member of a community of men who lived under religious vows in a monastery

Motive The reason that a person has for doing something

Motte and bailey An early castle that featured a fort on a hill surrounded by a fence or wall

Norman People from Normany, France, who invaded Britain in 1066 and were led by William of Normandy

Norman Conquest The invasion and settlement of England by the Normans, starting with the Battle of Hastings in 1066

Oubliette A secret dungeon in a castle

Page A boy, in service to a knight, who is training to become a knight himself

Parliament Controls the country and is made up of the monarch, the House of Lords and the House of Commons

Paying homage When a man publicly shows respect and loyalty to his lord

Peasants' Revolt An uprising where peasants, led by Wat Tyler, marched on London in 1381

Pilgrim A person who travels to a holy place for religious reasons

Pillory A wooden frame with holes for head and hands that was used as a punishment

Pneumonic One of the two types of plague in Black Death; carried in the air

Pope The head of the Catholic Church

Portcullis A heavy, strong barrier that can be lowered to block a castle gateway

Protest An action that shows that someone is unhappy or angry about something

Protestor Someone who takes part in a protest

Purging Making someone sick or go to the toilet in the belief that this would cure their illness

Rebellion A violent protest

Retreating When an army pulls out from a battle because they are being defeated

Revolt Another word for a rebellion or uprising

Sapper Soldiers who mined under castles in order to collapse the walls

Saracen A name for a Muslim at the time of the Crusades

Scavenger A person employed to clean the streets

Scold's bridle An instrument of punishment for a scolding woman; it fitted over the head and made talking difficult or painful

Scriptorium A room in a monastery in which manuscripts were copied

Scythe A weapon with a long, curved blade at the end of a pole

Shield-wall A long line of shields used for defence in a battle

Siege A method of attack where an army surrounds a castle, cutting off essential supplies, until the enemy is forced to surrender

Spear A weapon with a pointed tip on the end of a pole

Squire A young man, in service to a knight, who is training to become a knight himself

Stocks A wooden frame with holes for feet that was used as a punishment

Stone Age A period when weapons and tools were made of stone; it came before the Bronze Age

Tilt The barrier between jousting knights that prevented a fallen knight being trampled by the horses

Timeline A diagram showing events or dates in chronological order

Tithe The tenth of the food peasants grew that had to be given to the Church

Tithing A group of ten people who were responsible for each other's behaviour

Tournament A medieval event in which knights mounted on horseback jousted with blunted weapons

Trade The buying and selling of materials

Trebuchet A machine used in siege warfare that could throw large stones or other objects

Trencher A thick slice of bread used as a plate

Trepanning Drilling a hole in a patient's head in the belief that this would cure their headache

Trial by ordeal A way of letting God decide whether someone is innocent or guilty; common trials were fire, water and combat

Undermine To dig beneath a castle's walls in order to make them collapse

Vellum Fine parchment made from animal skins

Viking People from Denmark, Norway and Sweden who invaded Britain after 800 AD

Villein A peasant who worked for a lord in return for land

Wars of the Roses A series of battles between the English houses of York and Lancaster

Watch A group of people who patrolled the streets at night

Wattle and daub A medieval building material made of interwoven sticks covered with mud or clay

Index

NOTES TO HELP YOU USE THIS INDEX:

Kings and other royals are listed by their first name, so look for 'Richard II' and not 'King Richard'. Other people are listed by their surname, so look for 'Becket, Thomas' and not 'Thomas Becket'.

Great Clarendon Street, Oxford, OX2 6DP, United Kingdom

Oxford University Press is a department of the University of Oxford.
It furthers the University's objective of excellence in research,
scholarship, and education by publishing worldwide. Oxford is a
registered trade mark of Oxford University Press in the UK and in
certain other countries

British Library Cataloguing in Publication Data
Data available

978-0-19-839318-4

10 9 8 7 6 5 4 3 2 1

Paper used in the production of this book is a natural, recyclable
product made from wood grown in sustainable forests.
The manufacturing process conforms to the environmental
regulations of the country of origin.

Printed in Great Britain by Bell and Bain Ltd., Glasgow.

Acknowledgements

The publishers would like to thank the following for permissions to use their photographs:

p.8: jimmyjamesbond/iStock; **p.12:** Julei Woodhouse/Photolibrary; **p.14:** Ashmolean Museum; **p.16:** Bridgeman Art Library; **p.17:** Spanish School/Getty Images; **p.18:** Classical Numismatic Group, Inc.; **p.18:** British Museum; **p.19:** Dorling Kindersley: Kim Sayer; **p.30:** Michael Holford; **p.33:** Ancient Art and Architecture Collection Ltd.; **p.34:** Chetham's Library, Manchester, UK / The Bridgeman Art Library; **p.37:** Claudio Divizia/Shutterstock; **p.39:** The National Archives; **p.41:** British Library; **p.45:** AA World Travel Library/TopFoto; **p.45:** TopFoto:Woodmansterne; **p.46:** Eurasia Press/Photononstop/Corbis; **p.49:** Heritage Images/Corbis; **p.59:** Michael Holford; **p.60:** Adam Woolfitt/Corbis; **p.61:** Bettman/Corbis; **p.61:** Artyzan/Shutterstock; **p.61:** Artyzan/Shutterstock; **p.61:** Artyzan/Shutterstock; **p.62:** Patrick Cronne/Fotolia; **p.63:** Archives de l'Assistance Publique; **p.65:** iStockphoto; **p.65:** Mikhail Markovskiy/Shutterstock; **p.65:** akva/Shutterstock; **68:** Bibliotheque Nationale, Paris, France / The Bridgeman Art Library; **p.71:** Heritage Images/Lulu.com; **p.75:** Ronald Sheridan/Anicent Art and Architecture Collection; **p.75:** Clive Streeter/Dorling Kindersley; **p.78:** Bridgeman Art Library; **p.84:** Mary Evans Picture Library; **p.85:** David C Tomlinson/Getty Images; **p.87:** Mary Evans Picture Library; **p.91:** Private Collection / The Bridgeman Art Library; **p.93:** British Library; **p.94:** Fotolia/Richard McGuirk; **p.99:** Mary Evans Picture Library; **p.100:** Fortean Picture Library; **p.101:** Bodleian Library, Oxford; **p.101:** Bridgeman Art Library; **p.101:** Bibliotheque Nationale, Paris, France / The Bridgeman Art Library; **p.107:** British Library; **p.108:** London Aerial Photo Library, Ian/London Aerial Photo Library/Corbis; **p.108:** Ancient Art and Architecture Collection Ltd.; **p.109:** Universal Images Group/Getty Images; **p.111:** Cranach/Shutterstock; **p.113:** Mary Evans Picture Library; **p.114:** British Library Board/The Bridgeman Art Library; **p.114:** Royal Collection Enterprises Limited; **p.116:** Alan Gallery; **p.120:** British Library/Robana; **p.123:** The British Library Board; **p.127:** AKG Images; **p.131:** Mary Evans Picture Library; **p.132:** British Library; **p.133:** British Library; **p.132:** Bettman/Corbis; **p.143:** Mary Evans / Museum of the City of New York; **p.143:** iStockphoto; **p.143:** David G Britton/FreeFoto; **p.143:** David G Britton/FreeFoto; **p.143:** David G Britton/FreeFoto; **p.143:** Michael Owen/iStockphoto; **p.145:** Mary Evans Picture Library/DOUGLAS MCCARTHY; **p.145:** Corbis/Sygma; **p.147:** Derek Croucher; **p.149:** Mary Evans Picture Library; **p.153:** Nik Wheeler/Corbis; **p.157:** Society of Antiquaries of London, UK / The Bridgeman Art Library; **p.158:** Mary Evans Picture Library; **p.159:** Private Collection / The Stapleton Collection / The Bridgeman Art Library; **159:** FA/Getty Images; **p.159:** Dan Kitwood/Getty Images; **p.160:** Royal Holloway, University of London/The Bridgeman Art Library; **p.161:** Private collection, Ken Welsh/Bridgeman; **p.162:** National Portrait Gallery, London; **p.162:** National Portrait Gallery, London; **p.163:** National Portrait Gallery, London; **p.168:** Mary Evans Picture Library; **p.167:** Mary Evans Picture Library;

Cover illustration by Matthew Hollings

Illustrations by Moreno Chiacchiera, Jamil Dar, Rudolf Farkas, Tony Randell, Martin Sanders and Clive Wakfer

We are grateful for permission to reprint from the following copyright texts.

J F Aylett: *In Search of History 1066-1485* (Hodder Education, 2004), copyright © J F Aylett 1984, reproduced by permission of Hodder Education.

Modern translation of 'Sumer is Icumen In' from f.11v of *Harley Manuscript*, copyright © The British Library Board, reproduced by permission of the British Library.

We have made every effort to trace and contact all copyright holders before publication, but if notified of any errors or omissions, the publisher will be happy to rectify these at the earliest opportunity.

From the author, Aaron Wilkes: A huge thank you to Sarah Flynn, my publisher at OUP, who has managed this project from beginning to end. As the most energetic and enthusiastic person I know, she has always managed to smile no matter how ridiculous or unfeasible my ideas have been! In addition, big thanks must go to the brilliant Becky DeLozier, my editor, whose advice, dedication and practical suggestions have been invaluable. I must also acknowledge Janice Chan, Lois Durrant, Laura Syred and Fiona MacColl at OUP for their hard work on this project. I am particularly indebted to my wife, Emma, for all her support, patience and kind words – and to my daughters, Hannah and Eleanor, who always show an interest in what I'm writing and never look bored when I talk about it!

The publishers would like to thank the following people for offering their contribution in the development of this book and related components:
James Ball, for writing parts of the Second Editions of the books in this series.
Patrick Taylor, Director of Teaching at Chenderit School, for literacy consultancy.
Jerome Freeman, Educational Consultant, for assessment consultancy.